THE

CRAW*f*ISH

BOOK

Crawfishing in Austria in the year 1499. From Fischereibuch.

THE
CRAWfISH
BOOK

THE STORY OF MAN AND MUDBUGS
STARTING IN 25,000 B.C. AND ENDING
WITH THE BATCH JUST PUT ON TO BOIL

GLEN PITRE

University Press of Mississippi

JACKSON

Library of Congress Cataloging-in-Publication Data

Pitre, Glen, 1955–
    The crawfish book : the story of man and mudbugs starting in
25,000 B.C. and ending with the batch just put on to boil /Glen
Pitre.
        p.   cm.
    "A Muscadine book."
    Includes bibliographical references (p.   ) and indexes.
    ISBN 0-87805-599-1
    1. Crayfish.   2. Cookery (Crayfish)   I. Title.
QL444.M33P56   1993
595.3'841—dc20   92-38507
                                                                CIP

British Library Cataloging-in-Publication data available

FOR MICHELLE,

my heart, my soul,

my collaborator

CONTENTS

PREFACE

The Smithsonian's *Interdisciplinary Bibliography of Freshwater Crayfishes* cites 12,481 references. Why, like someone who can't push away a platter of crawdads, do I say, "Just one more"?

Allow me to crawfish out of answering for a moment and quote the great nineteenth-century naturalist T.H. Huxley on why *he* wrote a book about crawfish: "I have desired, in fact, to show how the careful study of one of the commonest and most insignificant of animals, leads us, step by step, from every-day knowledge to the widest generalizations." Huxley was speaking of biological science. I'm no T. H. Huxley, but even I can see that a look at man's relationship to crawfish does indeed lead to the "widest generalizations," though perhaps not so much about crawfish as about ourselves.

Object of study by philosophers of antiquity and today's scientific establishment, pioneer pauper's feast and gourmet entree of the Cajun food craze, key player in afternoon pastimes and modern aquaculture agribusiness, the crawfish has made generous contributions to science, folklore, cuisine and even music. If Native Americans and ancient Russians featured them in folktales, if Australian aborigines and Napoleon Bonaparte lunched on them to celebrate victories, and if blonde-haired Swedes and dark-eyed Cajuns use them to symbolize their cultural identity, then can the peoples of this earth really be so different as we sometimes pretend? The crawfish's place in astrology, medieval medicine and modern science attest to human beings' attempt to understand their world and live in harmony with it, while the crawfish holocaust caused by epidemics and pollution may offer lessons for our own future. A look at the crawfish business reveals price wars and trade wars, "mom and pop" operators and international joint ventures, anti-trust investigations and a thriving black market—in short, all the makings of a good case study in economics.

In the truth about crawfish lies the truth about ourselves, so let me offer, in the words of novelist Vance Palmer, "the truth, the whole truth, and no cray-fishing, so help me God."

Glen Pitre
Cut Off, Louisiana
Crawfish season, 1992

ACKNOWLEDGMENTS

To all the librarians whose halls my wife and I haunted, thanks. To all the people who took time away from catching, raising, processing, studying, promoting, cooking and eating crawfish to help with this book, I give an unqualified thanks.

To the following people I give a special *bien merci, beaucoup, beaucoup, beaucoup:* Sprinky Durand, who for ten years has gotten me into and out of trouble; to Gaywinn Gaudé, editor of *Crawfish Tales,* who was unselfish with her knowledge; to Drs. James Avault and Jay Huner, who with red pencil in hand took my manuscript and turned it into a better book than it might have been; Robert Romaire, for helping me avert the most egregious errors; to the folks at Louisiana Catalog, especially Katie Callais, who shield me so I can write; to my parents, for their usual (and unusual) patience; to my friends at University Press of Mississippi, especially JoAnne Prichard, who makes dealing with editors a pleasure; and finally to my wife, Michelle Benoit, who not only made this book possible, but who also makes it a joy to wake up each morning to the day's new adventure.

THE CRAW*f*ISH BOOK

WHAT'S IN A NAME?

IN addition to the scientific-sounding "crayfish" and the more enticing "crawfish," across America one hears many crawonyms: crawdad, crawdab, crawldad, crawdaddy, crawdabbler, crawpappy, crawjinny. Soft-shelled crawfish are softies, soft-craws or peelers. Some names such as mudbug or ditch bug, remind us of where crawfish live. Also evocative is the term "Irishman's friend," earned in the nineteenth century when crawfish burrows undermining Mississippi River levees supplied steady work for immigrant laborers. Other names are borrowed from crawfish cousins: land crab, grass crab, paper-shell crab, bay crab, creek crab, river crab, river lobster. The list is long, and so is the history.

Three and a half centuries before Christ, the great thinker Aristotle, who seemed to have opinions about everything and wrote them all down, in his classic *History of Animals* described a creature that was "small indeed as crabs, but in form resembles lobsters." When Rome ruled the known world three hundred years later, Pliny the Elder turned the tables, describing lobsters as being "like the crawfish."

Farther north, crawfish were similarly lumped together with their kin, sharing the names *crabba* (Old English), *krabbi* (Old Norse) and *chrebiz* (Old High German). From the latter came the medieval French *crevice* which would eventually become *écrevisse* but in the meantime followed William of Normandy in his conquest of England. Saxon peasants in conquered England no doubt resented having to use Norman words as much as they resented the Normans themselves. Remember how Robin Hood felt about Prince John! But since we can't all be Robin Hoods, the average peasant was left to subtler, less conscious means of undermining the overlords' authority.

Folk etymology, one of the many examples of humans trying to instill meaning where there is none, is the process by which words change into what people think they ought to be, such as the expression "metes and bounds" becoming the seemingly more sensible "leaps and bounds" after the mete faded from use in English measurement. Since the Norman's Middle English word *crevis* applied to a creature that lived in water, the English person quite reasonably came to call it "crayfish." With crawling its favored locomotion, the word "crawfish" was but a step away and, except in biology labs, it is now the preferred American form.

Now that that's clear, let's muddy the water again, for in some English-speaking places, such as Australia, crawfish are called crayfish, and in many such areas, what *are* called crawfish are saltwater lobsters! Some aborigines avoid the whole controversy by using sign language—they say "crawfish" by opening the thumb and index finger like pincers. Tristan da Cunha, a tiny island group in the south Atlantic, issued a series of postage stamps labeled "Crawfish Industry." One of them featured peasants in traditional costumes packing, and another showed them rowing out to catch—spiny lobsters. They taste just fine, but they're not

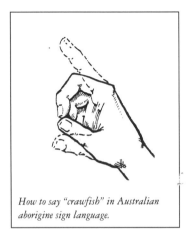

How to say "crawfish" in Australian aborigine sign language.

what Americans call crawfish. In this book, lobsters will be called lobsters. "Crawfish" will refer to the freshwater creature, except when quoting someone who did otherwise. If occasionally we refer to our subject as "mudbugs," it is only with the utmost affection. In reality, crawfish are not bugs and many species prefer clear running water with a hard, rocky bottom.

The word for this curious creature grew to accommodate other meanings as well. Backing out of a commitment, balking at a job once begun, even retreating from a battlefield are all actions described as "crawfishing," a reference to the mudbug's habit of swimming or crawling backward when alarmed. When young America was pushing west, full of fire and Manifest Destiny, trouble brewed over the boundary with British Canada in the crawfish-rich Pacific Northwest. Referring to degrees of latitude, "Fifty-four forty or fight!" became one of history's more curious militant slogans. A compromise placing the boundary at the forty-ninth parallel didn't stop freebooters from heading north. In 1848 the failure of one such incursion was explained to the U.S. Congress with, "No sooner did they see the old British lion rising up . . . than they crawfished back to forty-nine."

Moving around on one's hands and knees is also described as crawfishing, as are any of the many methods used to catch the critters. In the slang of World War I New Zealand soldiers, "crayfish" referred to a "contemptible schemer," though how the dull-witted crawfish earned that honor is cause for wonder. The crawfish generously offered its name to other animals (Graham's crawfish snake of the American midwest), natural features ("crawfish land," Ozark slang for swamp), and numerous places (from Crawfish Rock in Australia to Crawfish, Kentucky, to Crayford, England, to Ruisseau des Ecrevisses in France). And in the 1960s and 1970s, one of the bibles of American rock music was a magazine called *Crawdaddy!*

For one reason or another, certain persons earn the nickname "Crawfish." A 1986 *Wall Street Journal* reported the re-election victory of "Kentucky County Judge Carl Crawdad Sizemore." In Australia an awkward person sometimes wins the nickname "Yabby," after a local species. Among American Indians, Jeanette Langley reports that no one remembers how a fellow Coushatta got the nickname *Sok Cho,* "Crawfish."

The name has attached itself to whole peoples as well. One branch of the Choctaw was known as the *Chakchiuma,* the "red crawfish," another the *Shatje-ohla,* the "crawfish people." A group of Paiute are called *Go'ya'tikadu,* "crawfish-eaters." *Mon'shkon* (crawfish) was a clan of the Osage. Elders of Louisiana's Houma tribe still carve cypress effigies of their totem, the crawfish, which also served as a symbol of allegiance and identity in medieval Europe. In 1594 a crawfish appeared on the pennant of Conte Lodovico Lodovici of

Bologna. The Atwater family shield featured three *crevices,* and across feudal Europe armored knights marched to battle under banners emblazoned with mudbugs.

In today's world few of us brandish our coat of arms, but even with fax machines and Federal Express we do occasionally lick a postage stamp. Crawfish thrive in that territory as well. Across huge Russia and out from tiny Liechtenstein mudbugs have helped carry the mail. They've been honored on postage stamps in communist Rumania, capitalist Germany, fascist Spain, neutral Switzerland, post-independence Papua-New Guinea and third-world Cameroun, proving conclusively that the crawfish crawls above politics.

In the United States, the crawfish was put on a stamp commemorating the 1984 New Orleans World's Fair, but really the best places to catch one in this country are in music and literature. Hiawatha sings of them in Longfellow's poem. They crawl through the novels of Hemingway and the letters of Gertrude Stein, the folk tales of Native Americans and African-Americans, and even appear in children's stories. Crawfish are mentioned in many songs, and one of them belongs in the category of "best-loved American folksongs":

> You get a line and I'll get a pole, honey.
> You get a line and I'll get a pole, babe.
> You get line and I'll get a pole,
> And we'll go down to the crawdad hole,
> Honey, sugar baby, mine.

"The Crawdad Song" appears in scores of song books and has been recorded by many musicians, including Burl Ives and Pete Seeger. Another crawfish song, written in 1958 by Fred Wise and

Ben Weisman, turned up in studios with Harry Belafonte, Jerry Lee Lewis, and even Elvis Presley. But let's face it: whatever the crawfish has provided in the way of inspiration for singers and writers, the primary interest it holds for people is culinary.

You don't agree? You find yourself horrified by the sight of those crawly creatures? You wonder who could possibly eat those things? Crawfish lovers have included Emperor Maximilian I of Austria in the fifteenth century, Queen Elizabeth I of England in the sixteenth century, Tsar Peter the Great of Russia in the seventeenth century, and Emperor Napoleon Bonaparte of France in the eighteenth century. "Enough, enough," you say, quite rightly pointing out that none of those monarchs was American.

Even people who admit that great quantities of crawfish have been cooked in Wisconsin, ordered in Oregon, and savored in south Louisiana for quite some time often avow that in America at large mudbugs were forever and universally spurned. It's just not true.

From the bottomlands of Kentucky to the hills of Arkansas to the plains of Kansas, many pioneers undoubtedly forged the America we know today with the muscle and sinew that came from eating crawdads. After all, wasn't it on account of mudbugs that Nebraskans were once called "bug eaters"? Crawfish, which are numerous in times of flood, no doubt often saved from starvation those who'd watched their crops and livestock wash away. For conclusive proof, look again at "The Craw-dad Song":

> Get up old man, you slept too late,
> Last piece of crawdad's on your plate.

Like possums and coons, such a food might be cherished by those who have little and never make it to the plantation dining room (at

Crawfish stamps from Liechtenstein and Cameroun.

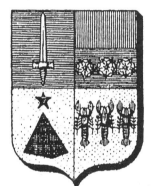

One of many coats of arms from medieval Europe that featured crawfish.

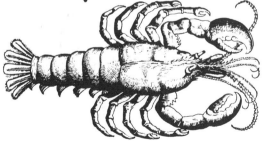

Crawfish by Conrad Gesner circa 1560.

The Crawdad Song (traditional)

You get a line and I'll get a pole, honey,
You get a line and I'll get a pole, babe,
You get a line and I'll get a pole,
And we'll go down to the crawdad hole,
Honey, sugar baby, mine.

Get up old man, you slept too late, honey,
Get up old man, you slept too late, babe,
Get up old man, you slept too late,
Last piece of crawdad's on your plate,
Honey, sugar baby, mine.

Get up old woman, you slept too late,
Crawdad man done passed your gate.

Along come a man with a sack on his back,
Packin' all the crawdads he can pack.

A sittin' on the ice till my feet got cold,
Watchin' that crawdad dig his hole.

Crawdad, crawdad, you better dig deep,
'Cause I'm gonna ramble in my sleep.

Sittin' on the bank till my feet got hot,
Watchin' that crawdad rack and trot.

Crawdad, crawdad, you better go to hole,
If I don't catch you, then durn my soul.

What you gonna do when the crawdads die,
Sit on the bank until I cry.

Alternate: substitute "this mornin', this evenin',
so soon" for "Honey, sugar baby, mine"

least not when company is coming). And unlike the hunting of those tree-climbing mammals, which can serve as a rite of manhood, there's little glory to be had in catching crawfish. Even children could (and usually did) do it.

Indeed, Euell Gibbons, the late expert on wild food, confessed, "The first edible creature I ever pulled from the water was a crawdad. From as early as I can remember, I was an ardent crawfisherman." He goes on to say that his grandfather showed him the best ways to catch crawfish, initiating him to the long-standing tradition.

Crawfish were not only eaten more widely than is commonly supposed, they were even peddled door to door—an early version of home delivery. Here's "The Crawdad Song" again:

> Get up old woman, you slept too late.
> The crawdad man done passed your gate.
> Along come a man with a sack on his back,
> Packing all the crawdads he can pack.

But crawfish were not only food for those who had little. They also teased the palates of the wealthy. Sold in markets of Atlantic seaboard cities at least by 1817, by the late 1800s crawfish were in enough demand in New York that dealers extended the season by importing them first from the Potomac River, then from Lake Michigan, and finally from the St. Lawrence River, chasing spring as it moved north.

Shipping crawfish is not simple. If raw they must be live. If cooked, they need cold storage, which in the 1800s meant lots of ice. In either case their transport must be expeditious, with no dawdling between loading dock and dining table. Before refrigeration and airplanes, crawfish shipped hundreds of miles could only be intended for well-heeled gourmets. In the 1880s, an eight-mile stretch of the Potomac River adjacent to Washington, DC, alone accounted for a half-million crawfish a year shipped to New York. Though no evidence survives, it's easy to assume that in the nearby capital, its cadres of crawfish-loving European diplomats consumed at least as much.

Across America, in season, crawfish clawed themselves into a market niche alongside lobster on the East Coast, crab on the West Coast, and shrimp on the Gulf. By the 1880s the crawfish industry had grown big enough for the federal government to take notice. The recorded annual catch was around seventy tons; but then as now, accurate statistics were elusive, and the seventy-ton figure almost certainly represented only a tiny fraction of the total catch. By 1906 *Science* magazine could report, "In New York, New Orleans, San Francisco, Chicago and other cities crayfish are sold both as food and as garnish, as bait and as material for school and college courses in zoology."

But we're getting way ahead of ourselves. The crawfish story starts much earlier—so early, in fact, that some say the crawfish played a part in the earth's creation.

ONCE UPON A TIME

W HEN the world was young, there was only sea and sky. All living things held a council to decide if there should be land. They elected the sun chief, and he let each creature have a say. When the vote was taken, they decided for land.

To create it, they would need a piece of mud from deep down under the water. A beaver tried to swim down and get it, but he couldn't go that deep. Then an otter was sent down, but he too failed to come back with the needed mud. Next a crawfish was elected to go. He didn't think he could make it, but he would not dishonor himself by refusing. Down he went. The others waited a very long time, but there was no sign of the crawfish. Finally, after four days, they spotted a yellow coloration in the water and saw that it was the crawfish coming back. The yellow color was the bit of mud he had brought up from the bottom. It was melting in his

Coushatta Indian crawfish effigy basket. Photo courtesy of Louisiana Country.

claw as he swam for the surface. Would he make it in time? He did! The sun took the speck of mud from the claw of the crawfish and cast it on the water. Thus the land was created.

Today the idea of crawfish creating the earth may bring a smile, but according to folklorist Earl Count, worldwide variations of the earth-diver legend make it "easily among the most widespread single concepts held by man." Around campfires throughout the southeastern woodlands, over the northern plains and in the Pacific Northwest, stories told about earth-diving crawfish helped Native Americans explain their world. Across the tundras of northern Asia, the forests of Russia, the plains of Hungary and along the Baltic coast of Germany and Scandinavia, "Earth-Diver" was told and retold, generation to generation, a piece of ancient lore handed down across the span of time.

Of course, the story varied from place to place. In many recorded versions, instead of a crawfish going, God sends the devil down to dive for primal mud. But if the devil steals the crawfish's role in the creation of the world, perhaps his dive at least explains the creation of the crawfish, for in Estonian tradition crawfish are fleas the devil shook off his back into the water. In Australian slang, "devil-devil land" is earth scarred with crawfish holes.

But of course not everyone associates crawfish with the diabolical. In Louisiana, the presence of many crawfish holes is considered a sign of rich soil. In Tunica, an Indian nation where the Red River meets the Mississippi, the word for "red crawfish," *kosuhkariya,* also means rainbow. According to Tunica tradition, the rainbow's colorful stripes are the face paint of a powerful medicine man. This shaman could lift crawfish and other creatures into the heavens, then drop them back at will.

Though that legend is ancient, the medicine man evidently still lurks nearby. In Marksville, Louisiana, site of the present-day Tunica-Biloxi reservation, as recently as October 23, 1947, live fish hailed down from the sky. (No, this isn't folklore. "Raining fish" really happens, though rarely.) While many theories involving updrafts and tornadoes have been put forward, scientists have never conclusively explained the raining crawfish phenomenon. But the Tunica have.

But what if it's not raining fish? What if it just rains, and rains, and rains? Crawfish are there, too. African-American folktales featuring Uncle Remus describe Noah preparing for the biblical flood by loading his ark "plum ter de Crawfishes." Stories of an ancient deluge are even more widespread than tales about the earth-driver. The Aranda tribe of Australia tell how the crawfish ancestor built a weir to hold back that flood. When the dam broke, the crawfish floated south with it, and to this day the crawfish-ancestor spears fish along the water's edge. Maybe that's why crawfish are thought

Tarot card. Note crawfish emerging from water, or "cosmic mind stuff."

to have predictive powers regarding rain. Throughout the United States farmers and frontiersmen have long held the notion that if a crawfish plugs up its burrow, they can expect rain before the day is out.

But the crawfish may have powers that go beyond forecasting the weather. In many versions of the tarot, playing cards used since ancient times for divining what is to come, key XVIII of the major arcana, the moon card, features a crawfish symbolizing the beginning stages of primitive consciousness. It is portrayed crawling from the water, and water itself represents "cosmic mind stuff" according to many guides to the tarot. Key XVIII is probably *not* the card you want to have turn up. Everyone agrees it implies deception in your future. The crawfish on the card represents the unknown, unforeseen, and unexpected. In the gloomy words of one mystic, the crawfish foretells "Danger. Scandal. Error. Disgrace. Dishonor. Slander. Libel. Immorality. An insincere personal relationship. Superficiality. False friends. Unknown enemies." In Ivan Turgenev's novel *Fathers and Sons,* a long list of proofs that a certain character was superstitious included the fact that she would not eat crawfish. Based on the tarot, can you blame her?

The crawfish earns its humble role in the tarot by virtue of its representing the zodiac symbol Cancer, which is ruled by the moon. But let's back up a moment. When the Roman Petronius, in his famous *Satyricon,* first noted the crawfish's place in the zodiac, it was the sign later to be known as Scorpio. That crawfish-scorpion connection had already been well established by the Greeks, who not only believed that crawfish (beaten raw and mixed with asses' milk) were good for scorpion stings but that crawfish prepared in a somewhat different potion could kill the scorpions themselves. And if, as the 1558 *Natural Magick* recommends, ten crawfish are ground up with a handful of basil "all the Scorpions thereabouts will come unto it." Maybe that's what happened. When all those scorpions showed up, the crawfish was overwhelmed and replaced, disappearing from the zodiac sign of Scorpio.

But the crawdad's an illusive creature. If he was bumped from Scorpio, he found a new home under Cancer, staying with relatives as it were, since to this day as bay crabs in Wisconsin, *krebs* in Germany, or *pak* in Russia, crawfish often share a name with their co-crustaceans.

The crawfish's new place in the zodiac resulted in continued enthusiasm for its extensive use in medicine. The reason so many mudbugs were ground up for potions and poultices was rooted in the "doctrine of signatures," which, according to medical historian James Young, was "older than Hippocrates, perennial in folk medicine, and given so much attention . . . as to seem like a fresh idea in the years that followed." In essence, the doctrine holds that cures exist for every illness, and as in some cosmic parlor game, God gives us clues by making the cure in some way similar to the problem it is supposed to correct. Young says, "Thus the thistle was useful for a stitch in the side, walnut shells for a cracked skull, and pulverized mummy for prolonged life."

If the crawfish represented the zodiac sign of Cancer, then perhaps it could cure cancer. Such beliefs are not limited to European tradition. In America, black slaves rubbed crawfish claws on the gums of their children when their teeth were coming out, and Cherokees did the same to their children's hands to insure a strong grip. The crawfish grip could also be compared to the tenacious bite of a rabid dog. Thus the ancient Greeks prescribed for rabies a three-day treatment of a potion of wine adulterated with two spoon-fuls of "the ashes of burnt crawfish."

Following this line of thinking, one can easily see how hard-shelled crawfish could be a real boon to dermatology. In the first century, Greeks mixed crushed crawdads with honey to soothe chapped feet. Before Europeans introduced honey bees to America, the Cherokees treated poison ivy with a poultice of pure fresh-ground crawfish, a 100 percent solution in the terminology of today's skin doctors. According to the World Health Organization, four out of five measles cases in a 1959 epidemic in Korea received the same smashed-crawfish juice treatment. If cultures centuries and oceans apart all rely on crawfish to treat rashes, one could hardly be blamed for taking a pole and a line to the nearest creek next time he or she starts to itch.

But crawfish also served as therapy for "muriatick and armoniack saltness" and "hectickes." The mudbug cure must have been quite thorough, for when's the last time you heard someone complain of those particular maladies? In 1714 in England John Purcell recom-mended "crayfish broths and garlick" to cure colic. By 1859 craw-fish were still listed in a French *Zoologie Medicale,* and an 1880 Ameri-can book recommends "cray-fish broth for purifying the blood."

All so long ago, you say? In the 1930s the Japanese were looking at crawfish as a treatment for tuberculosis. In the 1970s, Australian researchers were testing their potential for providing a magic bullet against cancer tumors. But then, why not? That's pretty much what the Greeks were saying two thousand years ago.

The part of the crawfish most useful in medicine are the two disc-shaped gastroliths that form in its head. Just as the human body stores up fat against future energy needs, the crawfish's body stores

calcium so that when the time arrives to molt and reharden, it has
a ready supply of the hardening agent to get the process started.
Known as "crab's eyes," gastroliths provided a thriving international trade during the Renaissance. Therapy for everything from
gallstones to bad teeth to weak hearts, the best quality crab eyes
reputedly came from Hungary and Russia. According to French
crawfish historian Marc Andre, "So many crawfish lived in the
Volga that great piles were left to rot by the riverside so Russian
pharmacists could use their eye stones." By 1533, works of *naturalis
historiae* regularly included accounts of gastroliths' curative proper-
ties. A typical 1599 text advises, "Take 6 or 7 Pickerell's eyes . . .
and as many Crevishe eyes" and grind with a mortar and pestle. In
Pierre Pomet's 1712 *Compleat History of Druggs* he too touts crawfish eyes.

In another reference to the theory of signatures, these same eye
stones were also thought to be useful in getting bits of dust from a
human eye. Finnish women are described using the gastrolith as
an aid in holding open a patient's eye while they picked out the
offending grit with the tips of their tongues. As late as the 1930s
Ozark hillbillies were reported to spend days hunting the best,
biggest crawfish in order to remove their gastroliths. Kept in a
pants pocket, such "lucky bones" were thought to prevent syphilis.
(Since syphilis is usually contracted with one's pants off, it's easy to
see why such protection often fails.) Lucky bones were also part of a
thriving underground trade in aphrodisiacs. If they worked, perhaps
it was because freedom from the worry of venereal disease improved
one's sexual performance.

The 1987 *Old Farmer's Almanac* recommends smoking crawfish
eyes in a tobacco pipe to cure toothache: "If the aching tooth is on

the right side, remove the left eye . . . and vice versa." While this remedy is likely based on an old cure using eye stones, not actual eyes, the almanac does not elaborate. Oh, well. Most doctors will readily admit that medicine is not an exact science. Once again, such beliefs are tied to the doctrine of signatures. A pair of disc-shaped gastroliths look a bit like eyes. To hillbillies at least, they resemble testicles. They could even pass for coins, and sure enough in Nordic countries carrying them in one's purse was believed to attract money. And if it can't be proven that crawfish bring wealth, at least it's well established all around the world that they're very useful for dispensing wisdom.

As the Maori of New Zealand say, *"Ka whe te koura,"* "the crawfish turns red in hot water," as indeed adversity changes us all. But adversity will hurt less and you'll get yourself out of hot water more easily if you have received the wisdom dispensed by your parents. As any parent knows, however, getting a child to listen means that the preaching had better be interesting. One way to accomplish that is to disguise the messages as games and stories.

Take the Russians, whose culture is rich with crawfish folktales, proverbs and riddles. Asks Mama, "What has scissors in its hands like a tailor, and thread in his mouth like a shoemaker?" Sometime later her child responds, "A crawfish does. His pincers are the scissors and his antenna are the thread." Little Ivan never knew the game was teaching him deductive reasoning. Russian tradition carries thousands of such riddles and the answer to many is crawfish. So deep has the mudbug burrowed into their language that he may crawl into any conversation.

If Americans describe a thing that falls between standard classifications as being "neither fish nor fowl," Russians would say it is "neither fish nor crawfish." One of that people's more fatalistic proverbs is "When the world goes to Hell, the fish will swim backward like crawfish." Considering that sentiment analogous to "the meek shall inherit the earth" would probably be stretching things a bit.

One fable, probably of German origin but certainly popular across Russia, invites comparison to "The Tortoise and the Hare." In "The Fox and the Crawfish," a cocky fox challenges a crawfish to a race. The crawfish agrees, but just as the fox starts to run, the crawfish clips onto its tail, hanging on over field and briar, until at the finish line, still undiscovered, it lets go and asks the winded fox, "What took you so long?"

The Ponca, Kansas, and Osage Indians of North America's central plains tell a story about a raccoon and a crawfish, usually recounted with much singing, but in *it* the crawfish plays the tricked instead of trickster. A hungry raccoon wants his younger brother to go with him after food. Younger brother rejects the idea of grapes, then hackberries, then buffalo berries, but jumps at the mention of tasty crawfish. To catch the crawfish, the raccoons play dead, lying in wait until a single crawfish walks over. He hits them and pokes them, but they make no sign of life. The crawfish leaves, then returns with his whole village, every one of which cautiously takes a turn kicking and sticking and shoving claws up the raccoons' nostrils, but neither raccoon betrays himself. Just as the foolish crawfish begin dancing to celebrate the death of the "shell-crushers," the two coons rise up and eat them all. The tale's moral is clear to young warriors whose success in the hunt or victory in battle may depend on stoic patience while they are waiting in ambush.

Among the many fables adapted from Aesop and Ariosto and

1840s illustration by Grandville of La Fontaine's fable "L'Ecrevisse et sa Fille."

rendered into verse by the French poet La Fontaine in 1668 was the story of the crawfish and her daughter. After a digression on the crawfish's backward walk as a metaphor for deception in battle, La Fontaine gets down to the heart of his story. A mother crawfish berates her daughter for her grotesque backward walk. The daughter's response (and the point of the fable) is to ask the mother how she can fault her child when she does no better herself.

The truth of the matter, of course, is that normally crawfish crawl forward. Backward locomotion is reserved for times of danger or occasional awkward swimming. People seem either not to realize that or to ignore it when in search of an analogy, as when Ambrose Bierce's classic *The Devil's Dictionary* credits Sir James Merivale with the observation that in the crawfish "human wisdom is admirably symbolized; for whereas the crawfish doth move only backward . . . seeing naught but the perils already passed, so the wisdom of man doth not enable him to avoid the follies that beset his course, but only to apprehend their nature backward."

Backward motion is only one area of crawfish folklore. The Cherokees thought that mudbugs came by their red color from being scorched by the sun when the world was created.

One burrowing species is known as "devil crawfish" or "deadman crawfish," because their chimneys are supposed to reveal where bodies are buried. Louisiana Cajuns call the same kind of crawfish *écrevisse tonnerre,* "thunder crawfish." If one pinches you, you better pray for rain because it won't let go till thunder peals in the sky.

Many long-standing legends maintain that crawfish caught when the moon is full are fat, whereas if there is no moon or bad weather is covering it, crawfish are skinny. No one has ever proved such a claim, but it's so widely believed that many theories exist to offer explanations. The eighteenth-century naturalist T. H. Huxley believed it was a matter of tides. Many a Cajun crawfisherman will give you this common-sense explanation: "With no moon, the crawfish can't see to eat." And remember the tarot card—the crawfish as astrological symbol of Cancer is ruled by the moon.

Some legends portray supernatural crawfish. It's true that giant crawfish are one of the perils to evade in the video game "Dungeons and Dragons," and crawfish inspired the fiends in the 1966 movie *Claw Monsters,* but there are also apparitions of much longer standing.

The Choctaws tell of a race of crawfish with whom they had a great battle. After the crawfish retreated to their underground caves, the Choctaws managed to smoke them out. Instead of killing them, the Choctaws treated them kindly, teaching them to speak, walk on two legs, and live like Choctaws.

The traditions of many southeastern Indian tribes include owl-crawfish specters that sometimes aided the lost but at other times brought destruction to those who ignored taboos. One young man had been warned that if he swallowed a crawfish and whooped like an owl, owls would come bite him. "If they come I'll kill them all," he responded, unafraid. That night, after building up a big fire, he ate a crawfish, then hooted like an owl. Immediately from the trees flew dozens of owls. Carrying water on their wings, they put out his fire. Then each in turn swooped down on him, plucking the hairs out of his scalp until he was completely bald.

Having your hair plucked may seem like harsh punishment, but it pales next to the treatment afforded poor crawfish by students around the world, who slice them open and pick at them, all in the name of science.

A CREATURE OF HABITS

F RESH out of college, biology teacher Louis Plaisance con-
fronted his first class of tenth-graders. At times he experienced
déjà vu, for not so very long ago he himself had sat in desks like
theirs, surrounded by their look-alike older brothers and sisters.
In the spring, like biology students across America, Louis's pu-
pils were to dissect crawfish as part of their study of arthropods.
Although most schools rely on mail-order specimens, in South
Lafourche, Louisiana, deep Cajun country, a teacher could extend
his materials budget by buying crawfish from a roadside vendor.
Though it was very early in the season, with a little searching Louis
managed to track down a forty-pound sack of the first crawfish of
the year.

Called to the front office about a minor matter, Louis left his students to choose their lab partners and prepare their dissection trays.

His business with the principal took longer than expected, and on his way back a cafeteria worker stopped him in the hall. "If your class needs more salt, tell them we have plenty." Louis nodded a quick, confused thank-you. His footsteps quickened as he headed for his classroom. When he got there, he caught his students red-handed, literally. Crawfish intended for dissection had been boiled and were being eaten in good Cajun style. Suddenly contrite faces froze in odd postures, crawfish heads pressed to lips, tails halfway to open mouths, and Louis realized that at this moment his students looked more than ever like their older brothers and sisters, maybe even like himself at their age. As if to confirm that notion, the class clown pointed at the row of lab table Bunsen burners where each bubbling beaker held reddening crawfish. "Don't worry, Mr. Plaisance. We saved some for you in the next batch."

The crawfish Louis's students ate were among the world's 450 species, three-quarters of them found in North America. Undoubtedly new ones await discovery, for the crawfish has proved itself quite an adaptable creature. A species found near Hudson Bay can survive extreme cold; another, the heat of tropical Africa. Some live in the inaccessible mountains of New Guinea; some in the shadow of casinos in Lake Tahoe. Still others inhabit the deserts of Australia, or American caves that never see the light of day.

In the heyday of the British Empire, explorers brought back news and sometimes samples of the world's far-flung crawfish. As with butterflies, naturalists collected crawfish. Beginning in 1839 they were displayed in the "Cabinet Zoologique" at the Imperial University in Kiev, Ukraine. The modern-day Rendell Rhoades Collection at the Ohio State Museum and the Horton H. Hobbs, Jr., collection at the Smithsonian Institution are famous. By the mid-

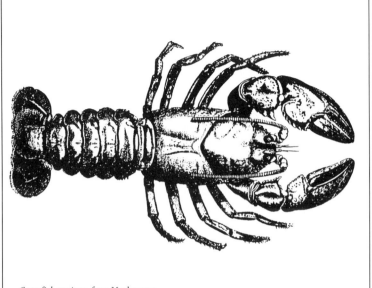

Crawfish specimen from Madagascar.
From T. H. Huxley's The Crayfish. An Introduction to Zoology.

1800s, Kessler in Russia, von Rosenhof in Germany, Sauvadon in France, Chilton in New Zealand and Faxon in America were among those studying the creatures intensively.

But the fellow who really transformed mudbugs into an ever-ready foot soldier in the army of science was T. H. Huxley, who in 1880 published *The Crayfish. An Introduction to Zoology.* None of those other scientists had managed to do what Huxley did—that is to equate in the public mind the study of crawfish with the study of the living world. Within a year his book appeared in French, then in German, then Italian; it became an international best seller. (A century later it was still in print!)

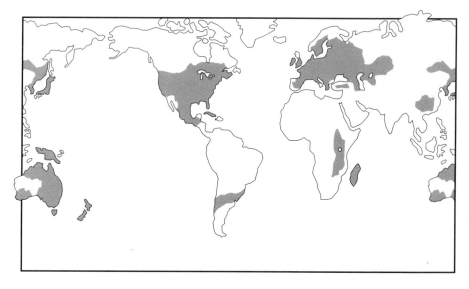

Crawfish-producing areas circa 1990.

Immediately astacology (the study of crawfish) became a hot
science. A regular column about crawfish found a place in the
American Monthly Microscopial Journal. The same year an Austrian
medical student cut his theoretical teeth on crawfish neurons, delivering his first paper to the Academy of Sciences in Vienna. The
student's name was Sigmund Freud. Not far from the same city, in
Hinterthal, Austria, ninety-one years later, the International Association of Astacology held its first crawfish symposium on subjects
historical, physiological and aquacultural. And around the world,
crawfish were still being sacrificed to the development of young
minds.

In America, most dissection specimens come from Wisconsin or
Louisiana. Twenty-five miles up the bayou from the school where

Louis Plaisance is now an assistant principal, during crawfish season Danny Kraemer works late into the night. In his back yard laboratory Danny prepares the crawfish that students across North America will cut open. Some are shipped out live, but many must be preserved. One by one, into a quarter- to a half-million crawfish a season, Danny injects dye to make the circulatory system easier to find. When crawfish season ends, does Danny rest? "I wish. But that's when I start on grasshoppers."

Preserved crawfish from Danny's lab and others like it travel in fifty-five-gallon drums to the supply houses that deal directly with schools. Such companies' catalogs offer not only actual crawfish, but also dissection guides, wall charts, giant plastic crawfish with removable organs, and (most feared by students) ready-to-hand-out crawfish quizzes.

Some people prefer to study live crawfish in an aquarium, an environment where they can thrive if given plants on which to graze and an occasional insect, piece of meat, fish food, dog or cat food, or chunk of earthworm for a special treat. Put down enough mud, and they may burrow for you.

Linnaeus, who between the 1730s and 1760s developed the *Systema Naturae* by which we still classify all living things, placed the crawfish (being a Swede, he likely lunched on them as well) in the animal kingdom's phylum Arthropoda, along with insects, spiders, and centipedes. Next comes their class, Crustacea, then order, Decapoda, where one finds familiar, edible crabs, shrimp and lobsters.

Further classification into family, genus and species, involves differences among crawfish, so let's stay for a moment with the decapods. This Latin word means "ten-legged," which applies to the

Scientific Names of Selected Species

(Note that not all classifications nor their spellings are agreed on by all scientists, and that classifications are occasionally changed to accommodate new discoveries.)

Astacopsis gouldi—world's largest crawfish, native to Tasmania.

Astacus astacus—noble crawfish (the name, not a description) of northern Europe, long the favored food species in such countries as Sweden, France, and Russia.

Astacus leptodactyls—slender-clawed or Turkish crawfish.

Austropotamobius torrentium—stone crawfish of central Europe.

Austropotamobius pallipes—white-clawed crawfish of western Europe and Britain.

Cambaroides japonicus—crawfish native to Japan, traditionally eaten raw.

Cherax destructor—yabbies of eastern Australia.

Cherax quadricarinatus—red claw crawfish, a darling of Australian entrepreneurs.

Cherax tenuimans—marrons of southwest Australia.

Euastacus armitis—Australia's Murray River lobster.

Fallicambarus destructor—Texas prairie crawfish of tractor-swallowing fame.

Orconectes inermis inermis—blind cave crawfish of Indiana.

Orconectes rusticus—"rusties," whose invasion of Wisconsin and Minnesota in huge numbers has made them a nuisance.

Orconectes virilis—crawfish of the American midwest which is sometimes caught for sale in Europe.

Pacifastacus leniusculus—prized signal crawfish of the American Pacific Northwest.

Procambarus zonangulus—white river crawfish of Louisiana and surrounding states.

Procambarus clarkii—red swamp crawfish, native to the Mississippi Valley and Gulf Coast and introduced to Europe, Asia, Africa and South America

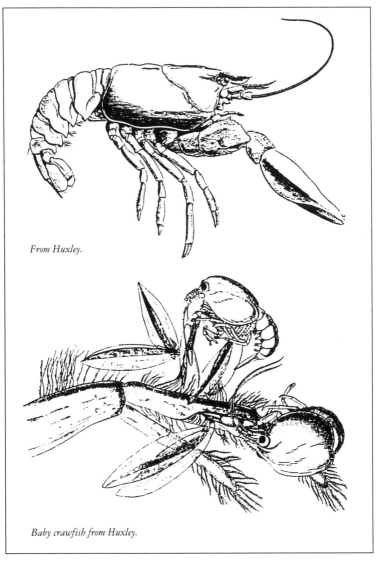

From Huxley.

Baby crawfish from Huxley.

crawfish if you count his claws. In many ways crawfish resemble their decapod cousins, crabs and lobsters. Tasmanian crawfish even grow every bit as big as lobsters. But besides subtle differences in anatomy and the fact that crawfish are aquatic (freshwater) and crabs and lobsters are marine (saltwater), there are dramatic differences in these crustaceans' childhoods.

After hatching, crabs and lobsters pass through a larval stage, just as butterflies must first spend time as caterpillars. Crawfish, on the other hand, hatch as miniature replicas of their mothers, and hang on tight to her swimmerets (the appendages under her abdomen) until they are ready to leave the "nursery." Of course their growth cannot be as straightforward as that of humans and other mammals who grow bigger, in flesh and bone, bit by bit. Like insects, crawfish have exoskeletons. The supporting structure is on the outside, with a carapace covering the "head" (cephalothorax) and linking segments over the "tail" (abdomen). Once hardened, the chitin they're made of can't be stretched or extended. Like a child's outgrown trousers, there's nothing to do but take them off and get a larger pair. This process, molting, begins with a new, soft shell forming beneath the old one. The crawfish goes through a series of convulsions, interrupted by periods of rest, until finally it shakes off the shell completely.

The crawfish is now vulnerable, a favorite of fish and therefore fishermen who prize "softies" for bait. It is during this time, before the shell hardens again, that the crawfish grows. To harden the shell, the crawfish draws on reserves of calcium stored in two flat discs inside it, the "crab eyes" or "lucky stones" so popular in ancient medicine. In a single season a crawfish may molt several times.

In Louisiana, short-lived red swamp crawfish molt a dozen times or more in the three to six months it takes them to mature.

When necessary, crawfish can also perform another type of growth, regeneration. If they lose a leg or a claw fighting off a predator, battling one of their own, or even in the process of molting, it will grow back until it is as large as the limb it replaced.

For all that growth, crawfish need to eat. And they certainly need to keep from being eaten.

The crawfish's niche in the food chain is both simple and complex: they feed on almost anything, and in turn they're food for almost anything. Huxley said it best: "Few things in the way of food are amiss to the crayfish; living or dead, fresh or carrion, animal or vegetable, it is all one." This lack of squeamishness is why crawfish were once used to clean skeletons for anatomical study, but Huxley may have overstated the carrion part. As any crawfisherman will tell you, mudbugs aren't drawn to rotten bait. And while they clearly prefer meat, their diet primarily consists of detritus, dead plant material that is covered with a living layer of bacteria, fungi, yeasts, and protozoa. But according to crawfish researcher Professor Jay Huner, "the small animals crawfish eat are essential to normal growth and development. Green plants are vital for normal coloration and healthy fat."

Great numbers of crawfish hatchlings are munched down by aquatic spiders and insects. As they grow, converting plant matter into crawfish meat, mudbugs' link in the food chain supports a diverse host of birds, amphibians, reptiles and mammals, including humans.

Sometimes it's a two-way street. Huxley recounts how a water rat (actually, a vole) "in search of a crayfish . . . is himself seized and held until he is suffocated, then his captor easily reverses the conditions of the anticipated meal." Crawfish will not only eat water rats, they'll also eat each other. Cannibalism is common, even to the point of munching down mates or offspring.

In the 1971 movie *The Ruling Class* Peter O'Toole beseeched, "Bless the crawfish with its scuttling walk," and indeed forward motion is not very rapid. Neither is the crawfish a very accomplished swimmer. When attacked, the crawfish's first response is to move out fast—backwards, hence the slang "to crawfish" out of a situation. Caught feeding, a crawfish while escaping will take its morsel with it. While that may be the mudbug equivalent of walking and chewing gum at the same time, they still aren't very bright. Measured neuron for neuron, people are more than one hundred thousand times smarter than the crawfish. Well, most people.

A hard shell provides the crawfish some protection, but, as Huxley says, "Claws are the chief weapons of offense and defense . . . and those who handle them incautiously will discover that their grip is by no means to be despised." In other words, watch out— they pinch and it hurts! To keep tabs on prey and predators, crawfish have retractable eyes that see quite well and can even distinguish colors. In murky water however, most information comes in through the various antennae, which smell, feel, and perhaps hear.

Females are marked by a small, round semen receptacle, called a "button," on the underside where the tail meets the body. Males have bigger claws, not one but two gonopods for delivering sperm, and little hooks on their legs to help hold on during sex.

Crawfish groom themselves. They engage in ritual combat with each other, establishing a pecking order just as dogs and cats and chickens do. And their mating rituals bear an unsettling resemblance to human foreplay. As in any Hollywood romance, courtship usually begins with a fight. After a couple of minutes, the male gives in and approaches with an apologetic strut. Male and female rub antennae, and often mouth parts as well, a crawfish kiss. One thing leads to another. With his mouth parts, the male carefully grooms the female's abdomen and button, then mounts her, belly to belly, in what, even applied to themselves, Russian lovers call "the crawfish position." Copulation lasts up to ninety minutes (for the crawfish, not necessarily the Russians).

Once burdened with the sperm of one or more males, the female mudbug starts to think about shelter. In burrowing species, this may be when digging starts. Tunneling down till she hits water, there she'll hollow out a chamber. The water is not to live in, for it's soon depleted of oxygen, but keeping her gills wet lets her breathe air. The male will try to follow her down, and usually he'll wind up hanging around somewhere in the tunnel.

To lay eggs, anywhere from a dozen to fifty times that many depending on the species, the female rolls onto her back for a process that takes several hours. It's at this point that each egg is fertilized with the sperm she's been carrying. The eggs look like a blackberry under the mother's tail, and indeed, at this stage she's said to be "in berry." The eggs will take two weeks to five months to hatch, depending on species and temperature. Mama keeps her eggs wet the whole time, practicing the crawfish version of pre-natal care. After hatching, the young hang on another month or so until they move out into the world.

Many times the most visible evidence of crawfish are their chimneys, sometimes erroneously called "snake holes." Rising several

inches above the surrounding terrain, the rough daubs of gray mud
that form the structure are smoothed on the inside to form an almost perfectly circular tunnel. The chimney seems to serve no real
purpose other than providing a place to put the mud excavated in
burrowing.

John James Audubon, the nineteenth-century artist/naturalist
whose *Birds of America* sneaks in a crawfish or two, recounts watching as a white ibis knocks a chunk of crawfish chimney into the
crawfish hole, then "patiently waits the result. The cray-fish, incom-
moded by the load of earth, instantly sets to work anew, and at last
reaches the entrance of its burrow; but the moment it comes in
sight, the Ibis seizes it with his bill."

Crawfish can be divided into two types, burrowers and non-burrowers. Burrowers spend much of their lives underground. Some are
rarely seen by people. Other burrowers, like America's red swamp
crawfish and the Australian yabby, are seasonal burrowers. When
it's dry they dig down to the water table; when it's wet they come
up. Non-burrowers, like the signal crawfish of the Pacific Northwest or the European noble, live in more permanent lakes and rivers
and don't do much burrowing at all, only digging in to lay eggs or
escape winter frosts.

To someone who has never seen it, among nature's most peculiar
sights are the crawfish migrations that feature thousands, even tens
of thousands, of mudbugs crawling up out of the water as if with
common purpose. In Louisiana in September, such herds are often
almost entirely elderly males enjoying a last hurrah in their twilight
days. In other seasons, they may be a mixture of young and old,
even females with hatchlings hanging on for dear life. No evidence
suggests any collective intelligence at work. There's no bull craw-

fish leading the herd, no Moses hunting for a promised land. No matter how large the group, each individual is reacting independently to the same stimulus, usually oxygen depletion in the pond they're leaving.

Where roads are built through swamps, sometimes the same oxygen-deprived conditions occur on both sides of the highway at once, prompting thousands of crawfish to cross right to left and thousands more to crawl in the opposite direction. Massive traffic jams of both cars and critters result.

In years past, such events prompted some south Louisiana towns to declare school holidays so students could take advantage of the windfall, but the phenomenon is not restricted to Louisiana. A 1981 Knoxville, Tennessee, newspaper headline asked, "Why did 10,000 crawfish crawl out of the water?" The 1985 Australian novel *Illywhacker* by Peter Carey mentions "the unsettling vision of yabbies [crawfish] moving from one side of the road to the other. . . . Squashed yabbies make the bush smell like the Sydney fish markets."

But at least yabbies taste good. According to the Houston *Chronicle,* the unappetizing, nocturnal Texas prairie crawfish "swarm at night by the thousands, crawl into offices, ruin farm land." Their eighteen-inch-tall chimneys, which can reach a density of 27,000 per acre, present formidable obstacles to farm equipment. When land honeycombed with burrows collapses, tractors "tumble into the caverns . . . and sink out of sight."

Some species of crawfish are cave-dwelling *troglobites,* blind, nearly albino creatures perfectly adapted to the dark, damp, steady temperatures of underground caverns, such as Kentucky's famous Mammoth Cave and Central Florida's honeycombs of limestone caverns.

Snow white is the natural coloration of cave crawfish, but sometimes odd hues result from genetic accidents. A common mutation renders red swamp crawfish a bright blue. Terry Guidry of Catahoula, Louisiana, reports that at peak season he'll see ten or twelve blue crawfish a day. "It's no big deal. They boil up bright and red like the rest of them."

Of course, some claims made about crawfish test one's ability to believe. "Barking crawfish" have been reported from Australia (probably a reference to the hissing of the Murray River lobster). Robert Romaire, a researcher at Louisiana State University, met a farmer who said he saw a crawfish straighten his tail and hold out his claws for two other crawfish to grasp as they spun him around like an auger. "I finally know how they dig them burrows," said the farmer, who claimed to have a video of the event.

His story is very hard to believe, of course. After all, if someone really saw three crawfish thus occupied, he wouldn't grab a video camera. He'd put a pot on to boil and grab a net!

YOU GET A LINE
& I'LL GET A POLE

POOKIE Poché refused to be outdone. He'd been crawfishing
for twenty years in south Louisiana's Atchafalaya Basin, and it
was only last season that he and his buddy Claybert Courville had
taken in Pookie's brother Nathan, shown him the ropes, and taught
him some but not all of the tricks. Yet Nathan was out-catching
them. It wasn't right, and today Pookie would not let it happen. As
dawn teased the eastern sky, Pookie's truck and trailer bounced over
a cattle guard on the one-lane road topping the levee that skirted
the swamp.

Pookie dumped his boat into the water from a muddy patch of
shore scarred with ruts where he and others had gotten stuck. The
day was dry, so his only worry was his motor. At a cost of $4000,
the crawfisherman was not anxious to buy a new one, but the constant starting and stopping, shifting of gears and bumping into

trees was hard on an outboard. He knew he was pushing his luck trying to get a third season out of this one. After balking once, then twice, the motor sputtered to a start. If it later stranded him in the middle of the swamp he could always make it out by swimming the channels and walking the shallows. He'd done it before.

The sky grew lighter, but it'd be hours before the sun rose high enough to be visible through the trees. Pookie, Claybert, and Nathan piloted their flotilla into successively narrower channels, from river to bayou to coulee to what's simply called a "run," just wide enough for the boat. Only a few scattered mud lumps affirmed that all the world was not as flooded as this forest.

The Atchafalaya Basin, America's largest swamp, can be described either as a cathedral of natural beauty or a morbid dreamscape, depending on one's comfort in nature's extremes. Spanish moss beards the trees. Cypress trunks bulb into delicate folds like gathered curtains. One monstrous tree that was missed when the swamp was cut over measures six feet in diameter, a reminder of what the whole basin looked like a century ago when the average cypress was a thousand years old.

Pookie and his companions reached the hiding place where they cache supplies, taking a calculated risk since nothing but concealment protects them from thieves. From the rendezvous, each set off to check his own traps, navigating by remembered trees, telling direction by wind and current as branches slapped their faces. It was the hard way to do things, but cutting branches or tying marker ribbons might tip off others to the location of their runs. Doing things the hard way is why crawfish buyers call men like Pookie and Claybert "alligator guys." They're every bit as tough as one.

Pookie had no idea who owned title to the flooded woods where he fished. The basin had always been open range. Nowadays some landowners were trying to extract payments for fishing rights, one of the many changes from the old days when one could fish the same area a whole season with a hundred traps. Pookie had a thousand traps. Moving them all to different fishing grounds ten times a season meant bleeding fingers and time lost from fishing, but it was necessary if you wanted to catch crawfish.

From a five-foot-tall trap, two dozen crawfish spilled into his bucket. By about 1940, before Pookie was born, such crawfish traps had evolved from illegal perch traps, which in turn had descended from hoop nets. Tossing in four fish (freshwater shad or saltwater pogy) and two pellets of artificial bait, Pookie dropped the trap back into the water. Twenty years of trial and error had taught Pookie when to set a trap upright and when to lay it flat, what size trap to use for what depth water, what size tree to tie it to, which side of the tree. So much to know. "If anyone could figure out crawfish, he'd be a millionaire," Pookie often said.

There was one old timer who'd been crawfishing sixty years who could lay a trap alongside Pookie's and catch three times the crawfish. Since that was true, Pookie should be catching twenty times as much as his little brother. But he wasn't.

"This is my last year," Pookie said, as if talking to the *gros becs* (night herons) roosting in the trees above. When he'd started twenty years before, a day's gasoline cost five dollars, bait ran forty dollars, and crawfish sold for forty cents a pound. Today, gas cost forty dollars and bait over one hundred dollars, but crawfish still brought forty cents a pound. Empty sacks were up to thirty cents

Pookie Poché catches crawfish in the Atchafalaya Basin. Photo: G. Pitre.

apiece. And with all the moving around, a seven-dollar trap barely lasted two years, less if a coon got hold of it.

Like seemingly every other animal in the swamp, raccoons love crawfish. They seem to take special delight in pulling a trap into a tree, smashing it up, then eating any of the mudbugs in it they can reach. Otters are more direct. They open the trap like a fisherman does, crawl inside to gobble up crawfish and bait, then go out the way they came. Pookie had figured out how to weave a trap closed with a welding rod, but what stopped the otter slowed him down as well. Perhaps the worst are snapping turtles. As they circle a trap, scared crawfish back up till they get stuck in the wire mesh. Then the turtle makes a second circuit, biting off the exposed tails. In addition to the fisherman's injury of lost crawfish goes the insult of his having to pick out heads before sacking the survivors for sale.

As he emptied another trap, Pookie wondered how his brother was doing. "This is no way to make a living," he says, "Up at four in the morning, fish till four in the afternoon, then sell and gas up and buy bait, not get home till six. Seven days a week, from high water to low." That's usually November through June.

It's lonely, too. Some husbands and wives fish as teams, but Pookie's wife had come out only twice, once before they married, once after, and she swore never again. Pookie's four daughters would all like to accompany him, but they were young yet.

The outboard motor missed, threatening to die, then caught again, *putta putta putta.* "My last year. Definitely."

But Pookie knows that if he ever quit he would miss the solitude and beauty of the swamp. He needs no license for what he does. No laws restrict the size or quantity of his catch. No one tells him what to do. The harder he works the more he makes, paid in cash at the

Century-old Portland crawfish restaurant.

Louisiana crawfish. Photo: G. Pitre.

end of each day. Picking up and moving on whenever he feels like it, he can fish whatever piece of swamp catches his eye no matter who claims to own it. He knows no regular job would leave him this free, as free as any American had been since the closing of all frontiers but this one a century before.

Peering through the moss-draped canopy, Pookie judged it to be about noon. He wasn't hungry, yet he was anxious to join Nathan and Claybert where they'd tie their boats together to eat cold sandwiches and discuss the morning's results. While his brother was still a bobbing spot of color through the trees, Pookie hollered, "How many?"

"Almost eight sacks. And you?"

"Nine and a half," Pookie answered, and smiled.

But one wonders how long the smiles will last, for the problems affecting basin crawfishermen are not likely to go away. The whole swamp is silting up. Earthworks designed to aid navigation and prevent floods hasten a natural process by which open water becomes swamp and swamp becomes dry land.

Where else to go? Pookie might suggest Lake Pearl, a little farther north, or in a wet year south near Pecan Island. But there are other crawfish waters, much farther away, that Pookie has never seen.

In 1962, naturalist Euell Gibbons bragged, "I have caught 500 crayfish in an afternoon from a lake that lies wholly within the city limits of Seattle." For those whose sense of adventure has a more culinary orientation, Seattle restaurants offer diners their choice of crawfish boiled with dill, beer or cayenne pepper, thus accommodating Scandinavian, Viennese and Cajun tastes. Indeed Swedes and southerners who came to work in the Pacific Northwest timber

industry get credit for the crawfish's persistent local popularity. In
the late 1960s, when an export-driven commercial crawfishery
boomed in Washington State, anger over hometown shortages bred
restrictions that all but eliminated the trade that had made mudbugs frequent flyers on Seattle-to-Europe routes.

Many Scandinavians settled in Washington and Oregon, but all
kinds of people were eating crawfish there long before the Swedes
arrived. Crawfish often appear in local native legends, and like
medieval Europeans, Shinook Indians deemed the broth healthful
for the sick. In the 1840s pioneers whose wagon trains rolled across
the plains and over the Rockies found that the Oregon Trail led to
crawfish. In the lush Columbia and Willamette valleys, the rivers'
tributaries and the surrounding sloughs teemed with crawdads.
Within half a century the area developed an important commercial
fishery.

By the end of the 1800s, Portland wholesalers were buying and
selling more than eighty tons of crawfish a year. Boiled in mulled
white wine and placed in iced-down buckets, the crawfish traveled
by schooner to Seattle and San Francisco and on railroad cars to St.
Louis and Salt Lake, where they were sold by the dozen or half-
dozen in the finer restaurants. In Portland itself, one of the city's
landmark eateries is Jake's Famous Crawfish, established in 1892 by
a transplanted New Yorker. A century later Jake's sells several hundred pounds of crawfish a week in dishes ranging from a cold half-
dozen boiled as an appetizer to Cajun dishes to exotic creations like
Crawfish Diana. Shipments from Louisiana often supplement local
supplies.

In the 1960s and 1970s many of Oregon's finest crawfish waters became too polluted to fish. By the 1990s cleanup efforts were showing results, but the center of the fishery had by then moved east, just over the Cascade Mountains, to the vicinity of Mount Hood. Much of the catch comes from the Warm Springs Indian Reservation, and many of Oregon's modern-day professional crawfishermen are Native Americans.

Al Smith, of Oregon Fish and Wildlife says, "Just like in Louisiana, Oregon crawfisherman usually have other jobs, or else are self-employed so they can take the time out. The typical crawfishing skiff is fifteen or twenty feet long. Fishermen use pots, like lobsters pots, sometimes made of wood but usually plastic. They bait them with fish scraps or dog food."

Dog food?

"Yeah, dog food," confirms Al. "The cheaper and smellier the better. Not just the canned stuff, either. Crawfish will come to the dry if it has enough odor."

A fifty-dollar commercial license opens the April 1–October 31 season (June to September is peak), with no limit as long as fishermen don't keep egg-bearing females or any under 3⅞ inches. Recreational crawfishermen don't need a license at all and face no closed season but are limited to catching one hundred crawfish per day. When fishing for fun, people use rings about a yard wide netted with wire mesh. To help the pro and amateur alike, Oregon State University publishes a circular entitled *Catching Crayfish for Fun and Profit.*

Pond farming has never been practical since local species grow slowly in the cool climate. Price fluctuations have historically caused wild swings in the number of fishermen working and the amount they catch. America's entries into World Wars I and II brought sharp drops in landings too, presumably because fishermen went off to fight.

When GIs came back from World War II, many joined the American Legion and Veterans of Foreign Wars. In the farming community of Tualatin, just ten miles south of Portland and smack dab in the heart of Oregon's traditional crawfish country, vets opted for a community fair to help pay for their new VFW hall. But every good fair needs a theme, so in 1951 the Tualatin Crawfish Festival was born. To the best of anyone's knowledge, it's the oldest crawfish festival in America. Delores Abernathy remembers that in the early days they'd fish the crawfish right there from the river, cook them in pickling spices and serve them cold as fit the local tastes. "In the beginning, the crawfish were given away. There was a free crawfish breakfast to draw people to the community. We'd sell fried chicken to pay off the hall." Nowadays the crawfish come from across the state, are bought ready cooked, and sell by the dozen, half-dozen, or, for the timid, one by one. The folks of Tualatin still work hard to keep their fest a family-type function; there are two stages of live entertainment, a parade, bike race, dog show, rides, crafts, and of course a crawfish-eating contest.

The same signal crawfish that supplied the Washington and Oregon fisheries and made Tualatin famous were transplanted south to California in the 1890s. They took firm hold in areas as diverse as chilly Lake Tahoe and the marshy Sacramento-San Joaquin delta. In the latter, the Louisiana red swamp crawfish had also been introduced and was thriving well enough to become a serious pest to rice farmers. By 1970 California's inland delta was home to an active commercial fishery that within a decade was dealing with a catch

Crawfishing on the Tualatin River circa 1890. Courtesy of Oregon Historical Society.

Red swamp crawfish. Photo: G. Pitre.

estimated at over two hundred tons. In a situation opposite from Louisiana's, a year of low-river levels means good catches and vice versa. To insure that most of the catch are two-to-three years old, California enforces a strict 3⅝-inch minimum-size limit.

Gary Florczak would love such a size limit, but his state, Wisconsin, has just the opposite policy. "The DNR won't let us throw the little ones back. I have to haul them to the bank and let them die. I wind up burying next year's crop." What concerns the Wisconsin Department of Natural Resources, as well as its counterparts in next-door Illinois and Minnesota, is the invasion of rusty crawfish that's pushing out the formerly dominant *virilis* and *immunis* species. Rusties, native to streams of the Ohio Valley, become incredibly abundant in the deep, clear lakes of Wisconsin and Minnesota. In huge numbers they're a pest in fish ponds and around areas where so-called "wild" rice is cultivated.

But Gary scoffs at that. He not only thinks the rusty is better tasting than Louisiana crawfish, he also claims they're better behaved. "Dump rusties in a box and they don't run. They don't fight. They just find a spot and tuck in their claws. That last sales trip to Europe, I'd go to meetings with Harvey in my pocket. Take him out, put him in their hand, you couldn't make him pinch. Docile as can be." But even Gary admits hard-shelled rusties "leave my thumb a bloody stump after peeling twenty pounds."

Gary and others credit Bob Pagle with being Wisconsin's "Mr. Crayfish," but Bob himself claims his role was quite accidental. "I went to Alabama with the thought to learn how to raise catfish. They told me crayfish were better for Wisconsin, so I went to Louisiana to learn what I could. When I came back to Wisconsin, they told me, 'Why raise them? The lakes are full of them already.'"

Though several tons of "crawfish" are exported to Europe, as much or more of the catch, referred to as "crabs," are sold as bait in Pennsylvania, Ohio, Indiana, and, until the rusty invasion made the trade illegal there, Illinois. Many bait crabs (a crawfish by any other name . . .) are held until they molt, since softshells are favored by both fish and fishermen. Facts and figures are scarce on an always rather secretive business that now keeps an even lower profile in the face of rusty-inspired regulations. Since diners want big crawfish and anglers want small ones, the two businesses would seem to be complementary, but actually the two types of fisheries are quite separate. Though bait crawfish bring less per pound, the small sizes desired are easier to catch and the market is always there. To sell crawfish as people food, many buyers must be educated on their value. Though nearby restaurants take some of what his eight hundred traps catch, Gary Florczak (and Harvey) make sales trips to Europe "because here local people are used to eating big chunks of red meat."

But things weren't always that way. In 1908, the local catch was recorded at 175 tons. Some of it got shipped long distance, but much wound up boiled and given away (presumably well salted) in saloons to help sell the product of Milwaukee's many breweries. Trade in this variant of "beer nuts" suffered when in 1926 Prohibition caused beer vendors, like burrowing crawfish, to go underground. When enforced temperance ended six years later, Milwaukeeans were so happy to have their beer back that crawfish were no longer needed to sell it. At least into the 1950s, Swedish restaurants in Milwaukee offered crawfish on the menu, not surprisingly, since Scandinavians in their native lands built a holiday (if not a cult) around the crawfish. Between the Civil War and the Great

Depression, one out of every four Swedes left the mother country for America. For Norwegians, the ratio was even higher. In 1900 Chicago had more Swedish-speaking residents than Malmö or Göteborg, more than any city in the world except Stockholm.

So why aren't crawfish as common as cheese in places like Chisago County, Minnesota; Bishop Hill, Illinois; or Lindsborg, Kansas? First, most Swedes left their homeland before closed seasons were established there, and thus well before opening day, *Kräft-premiär,* grew into a major holiday. Thus crawfish didn't carry a ceremonial value. Jeff Gunderson, a Norwegian-American fisheries agent in Duluth, guesses that the lack of crawfish tradition may have something to do with the economic level of the immigrants. Though the first wave brought many established farmers, later the typical Scandinavian arrival was a landless farm laborer or jobless factory worker. Back home, crawfish were already a rare and pricey gourmet food. Anyone who could afford a taste for crawfish did not need to leave in search of opportunity.

Just before those first big waves of Swedes came over, back in the early 1860s, in Louisiana the ancestors of Pookie Poche and Claybert Courville were no doubt eating lots of crawfish. Little else stood between them and starvation, for during the Civil War Cajun farmers found themselves plundered in turn by invading Union troops and camp followers, marauding Texas cavalry, and their own homegrown draft dodgers called Jayhawkers. During those same years, over in France, crawfish was such a popular gourmet item that efforts began to supplement the wild catch and imports with crawfish cultivated in ponds, an amalgam of fishing and agriculture that would not be seen commercially in America for another century. Even before that, helping nature along was not unknown. The

1662 *History of the Worthies of England* cites a certain Sir Christopher as "memorable for stocking the river Yower . . . with Crevishes." Sir Chris knew a good thing when he ate one.

In 1959 Breaux Bridge, Louisiana, was preparing to celebrate its centennial. By happy accident, a native son, Bob Angelle, was at the time Speaker of the Louisiana House of Representatives. He easily pushed through a resolution designating his hometown "Crawfish Capital of the World." Unfortunately, the crawfish did not cooperate. When an abnormally low natural crop caused embarrassing shortages, Angelle sponsored a $10,000 appropriation for a pilot crawfish farm. Some crawfish had been double-cropped with rice for at least half a decade, and state wildlife biologist Percy Viosca, Jr., had been preaching crawfish farming since the 1930s, but it was these latest state efforts that provided the impetus to expand the industry. By 1965, crawfish ponds that provided habitat for the red swamp and white river species covered 6,000 acres, and would blanket 115,000 acres a quarter century later.

It wasn't the kind of farming fellows who wore John Deere caps were used to. You couldn't even see your crop till it was time to harvest, and then you had to harvest over and over again for several months. It wasn't quite agriculture, so it was given a new name: aquaculture.

FARMERS WITHOUT PLOWS

NUTRIAS are 15 lb. rats, a favorite of the fur trade. They like to burrow as much as crawfish do, but naturally the holes are a lot bigger. One season, not too long ago, a Bayou Teche crawfish farmer flooded his pond right on schedule. Checking back the next day, he discovered it completely drained. He found and plugged the hole a nutria had dug clear through his levee, then turned on his pump to reflood.

Next day, drained again. He found the new hole, plugged it, and flooded the pond yet *encore,* as the Cajuns say. Next day, same problem. Running his pump so much was costing a fortune, so the farmer determined to get that nutria. He set traps. When that didn't work, he set bigger traps. When he started staying out all night, his wife began to worry, until he finally convinced her he wasn't running around, just staying put guarding his pond. He tried to get her to join him. She wouldn't.

When you're working "can to can't" (from dawn bright enough to see till dusk that's not), then trying to stay up all night, something's got to give. Eventually the farmer would doze off and the nutria would get his chance. Next morning, no water again! The farmer would growl a string of curses longer than the starter rope on that old pump. Well, as it turned out, crawfish were in short supply that season. Prices went cloud-top high. With a fresh change of oxygen-rich water every day, the farmer's crawfish felt so pampered they turned into the biggest, sweetest, most plentiful crawfish anybody ever remembered eating.

What the farmer made selling his catch easily paid for his pump fuel bill, *AND* a new car for his wife, *AND* a new garage to put it in, *AND* a dozen plump heads of lettuce that the farmer left out on the levee as a thank-you to that nutria with the golden touch.

Even without a Midas nutria, raising crawfish offers many attractions to a farmer. It's low tech and puts to use in otherwise slow seasons farm equipment and labor that are already part of overhead. True, crawfish ponds require lots of water, but in many cases that's their biggest blessing. Crawfish thrive on lands too soggy to be much good for anything else. Windell Curole, a former Louisiana Fisheries Extension agent, recalls many sugarcane farmers going into crawfish for just that reason. "In 1973, floods throughout the Mississippi Valley were even worse in Louisiana 'cause of extra-heavy rainfall. Old people started talking about the high water of '27." That was the worst flood in American history, leaving 300 drowned and 637,000 homeless and prompting Randy Newman a half-century later to croon, "They're trying to wash us away."

Crawfish farmer checks traps in his pond. Photo: G. Pitre.

Springtime floods have always been a fact of life in Louisiana. In plantation days, armed guards protected from sabotage the levees thrown up to keep the river within its banks. The same sentries stood lookout against "boils," geysers jetting up from crawfish holes that warned of an imminent break in the levee. In the 1730s, a colonial French (no doubt very bored) officer wrote a 4,700-verse poem featuring rhymes about repairing the seep left by a burrowing *écrevisse* (crawfish), lest a *crevasse* (flood) ensue. The 1927 disaster taught some hard lessons, and ever since the Army Corps of Engineers and local levee boards had been getting ready for a repeat. In 1973, their spillways were opened to divert the torrent. Even so, the Corps' Old River Control Structure came within feet—some say inches—of being undermined by churning water, a catastrophe that would have changed the course of the Mississippi River and left Baton Rouge without a port and New Orleans without drinking water.

Even after the day was saved at Old River, disasters great and small occurred across Louisiana. Recalls Windell, "When sugarcane farmers on Bayou Teche and Lafourche had their back fields flooded, a lot of them gave their neighbors the okay to go crawfishing. When they began hauling out crawfish by the truckload, farmers started to wonder if sugarcane was really the best crop for their swampy, harder-to-work backlands where the cane grew less sweet, less profitable. To grow crawfish, it seemed like all you had to do was add water."

But having a successful crawfish pond is more than a matter of flooding a swampy field. Many early efforts to recreate in a pond the natural conditions in the huge Atchafalaya Basin misfired. For example, in the basin, crawfish eat water hyacinths, so some farmers imported them into their ponds. But without the basin's free flow of water, hyacinths depleted the water's oxygen. Early ponds built on woodlands faced obstacles controlling water flow, tree litter, and harvesting. Marsh ponds were even less successful. According to crawfish scientist Robert Romaire, "Water quality is always the number one problem. When fish die, they float to the surface. Crawfish don't. By not monitoring water quality, people wind up scratching their heads wondering why they aren't catching any."

West of Bayou Teche lie flat prairies where thousands of farmers were already well versed in the management of ponds they seasonally flooded to grow rice. They knew a lot about crawfish too, and not only as pests. In California with its semi-permanent drought,

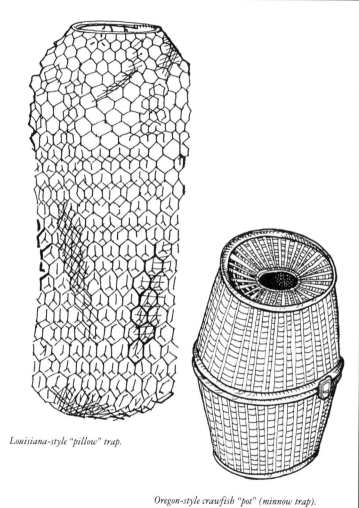

Louisiana-style "pillow" trap.

Oregon-style crawfish "pot" (minnow trap).

crawfish are a rice-field scourge because of water losses from their levee burrowing. In China, where each shoot of rice is planted by hand, the clipping of paddies by crawfish is an emotional outrage. But Louisiana gets sixty inches of rain a year. Rice is planted by airplane, huge acreages at a time. Crawfish *are* a nuisance and if plentiful enough can sometimes force replanting. But according to farmer Harold Benoit, "They don't seem so bad when you know how good they taste." After harvesting, Harold's father-in-law would reflood for the winter his rice ponds near Crowley. It helped keep the weeds down, and insured a goose or two for Christmas dinner and enough crawfish to eat at backyard *bouillitures* in the spring.

In bountiful years, "back before everybody was suing everybody else," he'd open his ponds to the public. Some people would pay twenty-five cents a pound, Harold remembers, but most would trade him half their catch. "It was a holiday atmosphere, especially on weekends. Lots of people with umbrellas and lawn chairs who'd sit on the levees, visit and crawfish."

Skyrocketing liability insurance rates eventually closed most southwest Louisiana ponds to the public (even though in 1990 the Crown Point Cat & Crawfish Club near New Orleans touted its "Two acres of virgin swamp offer exceptional opportunities for crawfishing"). But if the public was gone, crawfish were still there. Rice farmers were more interested than ever in growing a second crop in the same fields, but like their colleagues to the east they found that producing crawfish is not always as easy as it seems.

A crawfish's needs may be simple, but they can't be ignored. As with people, the first thing a mudbug demands in life and the last thing he forgoes is oxygen. Without it he dies. With too little, he won't grow. As Larry de la Bretonne, one of the early gurus of craw-

Louisiana logo. Courtesy of Terry Guidry, Catahoula Crawfish.

fish farming, often said, "It's hard to eat when someone's choking you." Keeping oxygen in a small, by nature stagnant, pond is no easy matter. Cold water holds more oxygen than warm, so farmers learned to resist the urge to be the first one with crawfish and instead wait until cooler October to flood their ponds. Floodgate baffles aerate water as it flows in. Plants that survive flooding are encouraged; others, like indigo, that don't are combated because their decomposition robs the pond of oxygen.

If farmers were the wagon train pioneers of crawfish aquaculture, their scouts were a cadre of Sea Grant Fisheries Extension Agents, comparable to the "county agents" associated with land grant universities. Researchers at Louisiana State University in Baton Rouge, University of Southwestern Louisiana in Lafayette, and other colleges led the partnership of laboratory science and fieldwork that eventually enabled yields of up to a ton of crawfish per acre and were instrumental in building what would become the nation's first major aquaculture industry.

Appropriately, if one believes that science should not be aloof, in 1974 LSU's Ben Hur Aquaculture Research Facility proved itself aptly named when it produced the winner of the big crawfish race at the Breaux Bridge, Louisiana, Crawfish Festival. Jay Huner, then a graduate student there, remembers picking out a medium sized female with small claws, so she would not be weighted down by larger ones. (Huner later went on to co-author *Red Swamp Crawfish: Its Biology and Exploitation.* More a layman's how-to manual than a scientific treatise, it marked a milestone in the effort to get the rapidly expanding body of crawfish knowledge out of the laboratory and into the field.)

The Louisiana Crawfish Farmers Association also helped spread information through its regular journal, *Crawfish Tales,* and eventually grew into a voice for marketing and lobbying. Both were necessary, for even with improved production, many obstacles stood between a crawfish farmer and a profit.

Predators take their toll. When flooding or drawing down (draining) ponds, a farmer must be careful to keep out fish. Many of the birds that prey most efficiently on crawfish are legally protected, so farmers hope rockets and butane cannons can make sufficient racket to harass them into leaving.

An Atchafalaya Basin crawfishman must catch enough to pay for his boat, his bait and his time. A crawfish farmer has the same expenses and more, for he must create an environment where crawfish can thrive. That means clearing trees and building levees, buying pumps and quenching their bottomless thirst for fuel. In 1987 the Louisiana Cooperative Extension Service tallied the start-up costs for a forty-acre pond: $65,547. Even if well-digging could be avoided with the use of surface water, even if a farmer already had a truck, a mower and waders, and even if he was willing to replace an efficient crawfish combine with hard paddling and longer hours, the unavoidable cost was still at least $35,000.

And especially in the early years, no matter how hard a crawfish farmer worked, no matter how good his science, whether he made a profit or not depended on the natural conditions in the Atchafalaya Basin. In a wet year, the swamp produced a lot of crawfish and prices fell. In a dry year, on average three out of ten, pond farmers could cash in, with or without a nutria with a "golden touch."

To cover capital depreciation and operating costs, farmers try to get more crawfish to market earlier in the season to take advantage of the higher prices before the basin crop comes in, but biology and climate limit their room to maneuver. Of course, some crawfish farmers shared the attitude held by the father in the musical *The Band Inside Your Head.* He gave his son an open-handed slap for suggesting they convert their money-losing crawfish pond into a soybean field. "Who ever heard of a Soybean étouffée?" he asked indignantly.

The typical Louisiana crawfish pond is flooded in October when spawning has peaked, and cooler, more oxygenated water coaxes both adults and hatchlings out of their burrows. Sometimes a pond is flooded, drained and flooded again to flush out oxygen-robbing dead plants. Harvesting begins in November (if there are crawfish!) and continues through May. In June, the pond is drawn down and by July is dry enough to plant rice, millet or sorghum to supplement natural alligatorweed and smartweed as crawfish forage when the cycle begins again with flooding in October. In ponds where crawfish are a second crop to rice, draining comes early, with the April and May mudbug harvest sacrificed to the planting of grain.

As pond acreage grew, getting around in them became a real problem. Pirogues gave way to "Joe boats" or "John boats," flat-bottomed skiffs Cajuns call *chalands.* Crawfish ponds are too shallow for conventional motors, so adaptations like "go-devils," outboards with their propellers on the end of a long shaft, were devised.

Around 1980 the invention of the crawfish combine suddenly quadrupled the acreage a fisherman could cover. Hydraulics turn a deep-tread wheel that pulls the boat at just the right speed to pick up, empty, rebait, and put back a trap before reaching the next one. A man who could check four hundred traps a day could do almost four hundred an hour with the combine. Louisiana craftsmen built several hundred such machines in the 1980s, often for sale to professional or semi-pro crawfishermen who'd trap several farmers' ponds on a sharecrop or cash-lease basis.

Improvements meant steadier supplies, lower retail prices, and thus increased demand. And if Louisiana was going crawfish-crazy, the madness was spreading beyond her borders. Cajuns had been moving to Texas for oil field work since 1902. Starting in the 1960s, high tech booms in aerospace and then computers increased

Children crawfishing with a lift net. Photo: G. Pitre.

the power of the Houston magnet. Newcomers refused to leave their crawfish behind. Computer engineer Philip Hall left Lafayette, Louisiana, for a job with a NASA contractor. After a decade in Texas, when he and wife Yvonne sit down to Christmas dinner, crawfish étouffée is still their first course.

From Cajun immigrants, the taste for crawfish spread. Each spring the seventy-five Arabian Temple Clown Jewels, Houston area Shriners who perform at parades and children's hospitals, gather with their wives and children to—well—clown around. When they elected a Louisiana transplant as president their picnic became a crawfish boil. Fluffing the coarse tresses of her husband

Mitch's Bozo-type yak hair wig, Betty Richardson remembers that after the Louisianan's year-long term ended, the clowns resoundly voted down a motion to return the event to its original menu.

Supply rose to answer demand. Texas crawfish farming began in 1979 when Amos Roy put in ponds in Orange County, just across the Sabine River from Louisiana. Crawfish aquaculture remains concentrated in the southeast corner of the state where many of the large Cajun minority still call Louisiana "the Motherland." Production eventually reached a full 10 percent of the next-door Bayou State's total. Friendly competition grew into "crawfish wars" in 1989 when Texas Agriculture Commissioner Jim Hightower held a news conference to praise his state's crawfish, and in doing so described Louisiana crawfish as "smelly, mud-coated, itty-bitty and slow-witted." His Louisiana counterpart fired back that Hightower "didn't know a crawfish from an armadillo."

The situation was less rancorous among private citizens, as Jack Hahn saw his home town of Spring go from "an abandoned railroad town to one of Texas's largest festival venues, thanks to crawdads and transplanted Louisianans." Jack credits the former for the crowds, and the latter for the idea of the Texas Crawfish Festival. Established in 1987, five years later twenty tons of crawfish no longer lasted the weekend as attendance approached 100,000.

Crawfish aquaculture eventually spread to every seaboard state from Maryland to Texas, and north through Arkansas, Oklahoma and Missouri. In each state, the industry took a slightly different tack, responding to different local conditions. In California's Sacramento River delta, as anywhere rice was grown, crawfish seemed a natural to farmers already equipped for pond flooding and also well acquainted with the pesky mudbug. A 1947 USDA brochure brags of killing 8,700 crawfish with a single DDT-soaked bushel of cottonseed. With ever-tightening pesticide regulations, for many, farming crawfish is a classic case of, "If you can't beat them, join them." As far back as 1902, Monroe County in the Florida Everglades shipped north almost twenty-eight tons of crawfish, but that was wild catch. In the 1980s, pond farming was a new enterprise, and as in Louisiana, was often seen as a better use of marginal lands where sugarcane grew less profitably.

In South Carolina, on the other hand, ever since colonial days farmers have built dikes to flood land for rice. Seed crawfish from Louisiana got aquaculture started there in 1976. As in Louisiana, early trial and error taught hard lessons, but also like their sister state, Sea Grant extension agents helped disseminate information so that pioneer farmers need not repeat others' mistakes. At first, the entire South Carolina crop was sold for bait, but in 1980 a resort town innkeeper and a local reporter helped start a festival specifically to promote crawfish as food. The South Carolina Crawfish Festival and Aquaculture Fair occurs annually at Pawley's Island, on the coast midway between Charleston and Wilmington, North Carolina. Lacking a native crawfish-eating tradition (at least not since colonials recorded Carolina Indians eating crawfish in the 1700s), the event borrowed Cajun dishes, Cajun music, and an overall Cajun theme.

Occasionally something was lost in the translation. One brochure offered "blackened crawfish" and portrayed Cajuns wearing berets and playing concertinas instead of accordions. By 1991, however, when the winner of the best recipe contest was "crawfish and wild mushroom enchiladas with black bean sauce," the festival had matured into a celebration unique unto itself. Along the way it helped promote a South Carolina crawfish industry that boasted a thirty-five-member growers' association farming over a thousand acres.

If supply bred demand in South Carolina, across the border in North Carolina it was pretty much the other way around. The craw-fish farmer there is typically not a land farmer at all, but someone in some other field (including at least one neurosurgeon) drawn to a sideline that can offer good profits. "Cajun yuppies" transplanted to cities like Raleigh and Durham drive a small but thriving mar-ket, where in 1991 the local Winn-Dixie asked $4.99 a pound for boiled crawfish and where at a Saturday farmers' market twelve hundred pounds of live crawfish could turn into $2,400 cash a half hour later.

Around the country, crawfish aquaculture research continues, with much emphasis on polyculture, the double-cropping of crawfish with rice, cattle or fish, even prawn/catfish with rice/crawfish rotation. One study proposes growing crawfish and water-cress on municipal sewerage, or killing two birds with one stone by fattening crawdads on otherwise hard-to-get-rid-of poultry drop-pings, salmon hatchery runoff and food-processing waste.

In Louisiana, efforts push better reporting of acreages and yields so that crawfish husbandry can become as scientific, and therefore as productive, as other food industries. Such research testifies to the ever-growing sums changing hands in the mudbug business.

THE MUDBUG BUSINESS

HENRI Boulet poles his pirogue over the mist-shrouded water, pausing to look when a flight of ducks rises from the next pond over. They voice disapproval at the invasion of their realm, but this is Henri's realm, too. He goes back to piercing the still water with his long *fourche,* finds the muddy bottom, and with a practiced shove propels his boat forward. It's a scene that could have happened a hundred years ago. With a change of clothes and a subtle transformation of facial features, it could be a thousand years back, when the first Americans plied these same waters, in the same type of boat, seeking the same food—crawfish. Later, after his morning's catch is sacked and cached in a cooler, Henri takes off his muddy boots and enters his bayouside house. On a touch-tone telephone, he taps a speed-dial button. A moment later, an air freight booker in Atlanta answers. Henri begins a familiar litany. "This is

Henri Boulet in his crawfish pond. Photo: G. Pitre.

Boulet Export. I have ten pieces going to Frankfurt, Germany, weighing in at 180 kilos, consisting of live crawfish. The airway bill—what? Sorry, live crayfish."

Louisiana's large-scale, mostly Cajun-run commercial crawfishery that people like Henri Boulet are steering down the bayou and into the twenty-first century does not have such a long history. True, crawfish had been sold in New Orleans markets for two centuries. True, local saloons like their counterparts in Milwaukee, Portland and other places had often used free crawfish as a draw. During the

Great Depression, peeling crawfish for bisque helped make ends meet for people in towns upriver from New Orleans.

But such markets were small-scale and haphazardly organized. If as early as the 1930s crawfish were on the springtime menu of the Hebert Hotel in Breaux Bridge, it was because Mr. Hebert knew he had a swamp not far from his doorstep, not because of any established regional supply network.

Beginning in the late 1940s along a strip between upper Bayou Teche and the Atchafalaya Basin, a string of villages became crawfish towns. Catahoula hosted the first peeling plant in 1949. Breaux Bridge was designated by the 1959 Louisiana legislature as "Crawfish Capital of the World." When in 1973 Interstate 10 arrived in Henderson, where there was already a thriving crawfish trade, a cluster of soon-to-be world-famous restaurants appeared. East of the basin, communities like Pierre Part, Bayou Pigeon and Belle River became crawfish centers as well.

In Catahoula, Sydney Guidry grew up on crawfish gumbo and crawfish pie. Not only was he around before blackened redfish, he even predates the invention of crawfish étouffée. Around 1950, on his days off from a dragline job, Sydney (locally pronounced Seed-NAY) started buying crawfish at three cents a pound, then driving twenty miles to Lafayette where he'd sell them for six cents a pound. If he over-purchased, he'd wind up giving his surplus away to some lucky stranger. "Bookkeeping was easy," he remembers. "I bought out of my left pocket, and I sold into my right pocket." Business grew more complicated when, within the decade, Sydney became the state's seventh licensed crawfish peeler, following the lead of local pioneers like Abby Latiolais, who'd got the very first license in 1949. Building up from a kitchen-table operation, Sydney eventually passed the reins to Sydney, Jr., better known around Catahoula as Peewee.

By the 1990s Peewee was buying from sixty fishermen each season, a third of whom sell only to him. "Those are the pros. Every year you know they're going to catch so much. You can put it in the book before the season starts." Loyalty is rewarded in times of surplus, for Peewee buys his regulars' catch when the more fickle fishermen find themselves scrambling to find a taker. Except for the extensive black market, consisting of roadside stands and sales to friends and neighbors, both wild catch and pond crawfish are sold to dealers like Peewee and his cousin Terry, who has his own plant, Catahoula Crawfish, just down the road.

Though a dealer's greatest volume is usually selling some live, some boiled to the public, Terry remembers his dad putting up jars of peeled crawfish for area restaurants. Now, parboiled and peeled product winds up in chilled or frozen one-pound packs. As much or more is sold in supermarkets as goes to restaurants. To fill orders, Terry's forty or so peelers work about ten hours a week in January, twice that in February, and forty to fifty hours a week when the season really kicks in from March through May.

In 1958 the New Orleans *Times-Picayune* described a crawfish-peeling device put together from old washing machine ringers as "the greatest invention since the cotton gin," but that contraption quickly faded from sight, as have countless others. Thus peeling is still done by hand, mostly by women, white, black and southeast Asian. Across the long, specially built tables one can hear snatches of English, Cajun French, lilting Creole and musical Laotian. But conversations are brief. The workers are paid by the pound, and

Peelers at work. Photo: G. Pitre.

taped-up fingers peel at a fast, steady pace. A good peeler can do a dozen crawfish a minute. In 1987 the IRS ruled such peelers to be regular employees, requiring withheld taxes and social security contributions. Even so, workers still show up when and only as often as they choose, and employers hire them only when they are needed.

The growth of the crawfish-peeling industry and increasing environmental concerns have resulted in attention to the 85 percent of the crawfish that is waste. Finding new uses for that waste help processors underwrite the costs of hauling it away. One plant extracts astaxanthin, the pigment that turns boiled shellfish red. In Japan, where artificial food coloring is prohibited, crawfish-extracted dye helps make processed fish look like crab meat. Fed to pond-raised salmon, it gives their meat the appropriate pink color lacking in fish raised in captivity. Other crawfish waste feeds mink, catfish, and even goes into commercial crawfish bait, though the latter is largely a grain product, composed of stuff such as barge sweepings. Freddie Hebert of Cameron, Louisiana, turns crawfish waste into methane gas which he then burns for energy. His pilot plant was paid for with federal and state grants, but he says the apparatus is based on his daddy's moonshine still.

Environmentalists and the IRS were not the only ones looking at the mudbug business. By the 1980s, health regulators halted the practice of giving paper cartons of crawfish fat (actually hepatopancreas) as lagniappe (Cajun for "something extra") with purchases of tail meat. And when Reagan-era policy decreed relaxed oversight of big corporate mergers, the crawfish industry provided anti-trust investigators with smaller game. Allan "Sprinky" Durand, an attorney for several Louisiana processors, scoffs at allegations of market-rigging in such a fragmented, "mom and pop" business. "Even if they *wanted* to fix the price, those crawfish people are too hard-headed to ever agree on what it'd be." Sprinky was part of a venture that in 1985 broke new ground by getting crawfish onto the menus of such national brew-and-burger chains as Bennigan's. Those sales died with the waning of the 1980s Cajun food craze. "They did fine with fried tails," Sprinky remembers, "but they didn't have the finesse for other recipes."

Such finesse is important. Many peeling plants were started by restauranteurs or seafood retailers in order to help guarantee quality and a steady supply in years of shortage. By the 1980s, many restaurants began to freeze crawfish during peak season so that they could offer them on the menu year-round. By the 1990s, speculators with huge freezers were warehousing tail meat to resell in late summer-early fall when prices were highest.

Henderson, at the west end of an eighteen-mile-long bridge that spans the interstate over the Atchafalaya Basin, became a node where a half-dozen large restaurants, all specializing in crawfish, grew up for a trade geared specifically to out-of-towners. According to Lionel Robin, who opened Robin's in 1974 and whose father had been a local restauranteur since the 1940s, hometown customers are definitely not what keeps area restaurants going. "Henderson has three thousand restaurant seats but only nine hundred registered voters." Lionel believes that Henderson's restaurants are valuable to the crawfish business not so much because of the actual crawfish sold, though the amount is considerable, but because of the promotional service rendered in acquainting tourists with the delights of properly cooked crawfish.

Lionel not only makes crawfish étouffée to serve in his own restaurant, he will "cook it, can it, freeze it and ship it" to anyone, individuals or other restaurants. While Lionel deals in multi-portion cans, largely geared toward institutions, others have developed single-serving portions attractively packaged for supermarket sales, crawfish quick-gourmet dinners. The intended market is not only convenience-minded Cajuns, but also others who like crawfish and may have been intimidated by the idea of cooking them.

In the 1980s, interest developed in soft-shelled crawfish, just-molted creatures that haven't yet rehardened. Long used as bait, soft crawfish drew interest not only as a novelty with wide-ranging culinary possibilities, but also because they're by weight 70 to 92 percent edible, compared to a 12 to 18 percent meat yield with hard crawfish. Lying low during that highly vulnerable stage, soft crawfish don't feed, and thus are rarely seen in bait traps, but picking out soon-to-molt crawfish and then keeping them in holding tanks till they shed is much like the process that has long proved profitable with soft-shelled crabs.

Low start-up costs and promises of profits of two to three dollars per pound over costs enticed as many as 175 operators into the business in the 1980s, but within a few years the industry shook out to a couple of dozen survivors who sell to restaurants worldwide. Softies sold in blister packs, ready for tempura, are even chipping away at Japan's resistance to crawfish. Of course, most soft-shelled crawfish sold go to lure fish, not people. U.S. Patent 4,646,464 was granted to a device to harness a crawfish to a fish hook. The Wisconsin crawfishery in particular has long catered to producers of soft-shells from Illinois to Pennsylvania, who in turn supply bait shops.

There is also a steady market for the crawfish used as biological specimens students learn to dissect and even a minor pet shop trade for aquariums, but those markets are mature. Their sales are flat. If sales growth comes, for soft crawfish and hard, it will be in the food industry, not just in Louisiana but around the country.

Though many tourists who've stopped to eat in Henderson have happy memories, easily three-quarters of Louisiana crawfish go for local consumption, especially during the forty days of Lent that start at midnight on Mardi Gras and end with Easter. Good Friday, when many of the mostly Roman Catholic population still observe fasts (of meat, not crawfish), is far and away the biggest sales day of the year. Come the following Monday, crawfish prices drop ten to fifteen cents a pound.

In Louisiana, crawfish marketing efforts by the Wildlife and Fisheries Commission were eventually split off to form a Crawfish Research and Promotion Board under the state's department of agriculture. That somewhat rancorous schism was more than a bureaucratic turf battle. It reflected policy makers' recognition that the crawfish trade was changing from the minor fishery it had always been to the substantial agribusiness it was quickly becoming.

From the beginning, however, crawfish marketing was largely the province of entrepreneurs. The 1958 movie *King Creole* begins with Elvis Presley walking onto his New Orleans French Quarter balcony to turn a passing street vendor's chant into a moving a cappella duet: "Crawfish, crawfish, . . . If you fry him crisp or boil him right, he'll be sweeter than sugar with every bite."

A song like that could attract anyone within earshot (especially with Elvis singing it!) but larger-scale promotion required financial investment by established seafood dealers. Prominent among them is Al Scramuzza, credited by many (including himself) with almost single-handedly raising crawfish from its previous status in New Orleans of, on the one hand, precious ingredient in bisque served to a vanishing race of upper-class Creoles, and on the other, a very occasional macho feast enjoyed by the patrons of neighborhood taverns.

In 1951, when Al bought his first eight sacks of Pierre Part crawfish, marked them up two cents a pound, and put them in the display case with the usual shrimp, crabs, fish and oysters, "it was unheard of." A year later, faced with a temporary overstock, Al "went out to a hardware store, bought three tubs, and came back and boiled them. In those days, the only place you could buy even crabs boiled was in a restaurant. Selling crawfish already boiled created a sensation." A natural showman, Al began local TV advertising in 1960, beginning with a spot in which, to the tune of "The Blue Danube," elegantly dressed twin blonde beauties demurely refuse a tuxedoed waiter's offers of steak and then pheasant, but jump up and start dancing when Al Scramuzza arrives with a platter of boiled crawfish. Remembers Al, "Next day the store was packed."

Promoting crawfish as served-whole party food, however, doesn't do much for the trade in more easily shipped and stored, higher-value-added, peeled tail meat. Marketing problems rooted in maintaining year-round supplies and prices competitive with other seafoods pale beside the battle to convince "the housewife in Indiana" that crawfish are good to eat. Few seafood dealers have the unforgettable face or pitchman's flair of Al Scramuzza.

Marketers frustrated by having to educate American consumers happily turn their attention to western Europe, whose well-heeled connoisseurs already consider crawfish a gourmet item and where a fine restaurant will often encircle a fish filet with three or four crawfish. Foreign trade, however, is fraught with pitfalls, as regulations on crawfish provide sniper fire in international trade wars. France banned the importation of live American crawfish in the mid-1980s. Switzerland followed a few years later. In Germany, to get American crawfish on the menu restauranteurs must sign an affidavit swearing they will not sell them as pets.

And of course, if Henri Boulet can sell his catch to foreigners, so foreigners can sell theirs in America. By 1992, the darkest cloud over Louisiana ponds was the arrival of low-cost crawfish meat from China. Rigid enforcement of product-labeling laws stalled but did not stop its entry into the market.

Information was hard to come by on a Chinese crawfish industry that seemed to spring full blown onto the scene. Chinese consular offices referred inquiries to other consular offices, round-robin. The Houston-based company reputed to be the largest importer had an unlisted phone number. In such a climate, rumors flew. Long-standing buyer-seller relationships threatened to pull asunder as peeling-plant operators accused restaurant chains of "buying Chinese tails on the sly."

The answer to such competition? According to Wendell Lorio, with Fisheries Extension Services at Louisiana State University, "Farmers will have to learn to produce a bigger crawfish." The industry has a long way to go before geneticists will be breeding larger crawfish as they do sweeter corn or faster horses. In warm

Baboo and Judy Guidry with crawfish packaged for Sweden. Photo: G. Pitre.

Louisiana, crawfish mature quickly. Getting them to grow bigger means keeping them amply supplied with food, oxygen and space. Overcrowded crawfish are stunted crawfish.

The desire for big crawfish gained impetus in the mid-1980s when Swedish buyers began arriving in Louisiana. Swedes pay top dollar for what is the centerpiece of their annual Crayfish Premiere holiday each August, but the crawfish must be clean, large, perfect specimens. The Swedes got there just in time, because after 1982 Louisiana's oil boom became the oil glut. A pound of peeled crawfish could buy a barrel of oil, and you'd get back change. Such jokes soon seemed less funny as plummeting incomes and dust bowl-style out-migration sent crawfish sales chasing the price of oil—down, down, down. With their own stocks long since depleted, Swedes, Finns and Norwegians had imported crawfish from Russia, Poland, Turkey, Oregon, Wisconsin and finally Louisiana. They were fickle buyers in their relentless search for steady supplies and consistent quality.

Before the arrival of the Swedes, in Louisiana crawfish were crawfish, so much a pound. With the Swedes only wanting the biggest ones, most buyers, even those whose only contact with the Swedish market was through middlemen, invested in mechanical grading equipment. Using such machines meant that no extra effort was required to refine the division further into #1 selects, #2 mediums, #3 peeling size and smaller rejects, which are sometimes used as brood stock for new ponds.

In the 1992 season, Breaux Bridge Export was one of the Louisiana plants freezing whole crawfish in dill sauce for the Swedish market. Owner/manager Baboo Guidry, whose blue eyes match

Packing crawfish at Breaux Bridge Export for sale in Sweden. Photo: G. Pitre.

his blue seersucker jumpsuit, carefully oversees every step of operations. Workers wear white coats and plastic caps as they carefully arranged boiled crawfish into one-kilo trays. Though the crawfish have been culled at least twice before, an on-site inspector from Sweden looks at every package, often rejecting a crawfish with a missing leg or eye, mismatched claws or a not-quite-perfect curl to the tail. "When you pay what the Swedes pay for crawfish," stresses Baboo, "you expect perfection." Baboo grew up on crawfish spiced with cayenne pepper, but nowadays he has whole fields of dill grown to order so that, once it's passed inspection, the tray is flooded with dill sauce to suit Scandinavian tastes, sealed, and then flash-frozen.

When enough boxes accumulate, a truck backs a reefer (a refrigerator trailer) up to the plant. A container loaded with eleven tons of dilled crawfish travels by interstate to the docks of Houston or New Orleans, is loaded onto a ship, and arrives in Göteborg three weeks later. Baboo shipped twenty such containers to Sweden in 1991. His local competitors sent about a hundred more.

Baboo relates that his Swedish partners are looking into peeled crawfish prepacked on crackers and even crawfish and cheese paste in toothpaste-style tubes, but for the foreseeable future most of the market will be for crawfish boiled in dill sauce and served whole, the way Swedes prefer the 12 million crawfish a year they consume beginning each August 8.

CRUSTACEANS OF MANY NATIONS

CAREFULLY, very carefully little Kicki raised the pole. She knew her brother was watching and that he thought her far too young for such important duty.

"Hold the lantern steady," she told him, trying to sound confident.

Just as Papa had taught her, she lifted with a strong steady motion until the *håv,* a ring of net, bubbled through the water to the surface. At its center, still chewing the bait, were three fat *kräftor.* From the corner of her eye Kicki looked to her brother and couldn't resist a smile when she saw she'd impressed him. Out on the broad river, bouncing lights marked where Papa and the other men had rowed to set larger traps. Too bad, Kicki thought. I'd love for Papa to see what I've caught. But this was August 8, Kicki's favorite day of the year except Christmas, and everyone was busy with preparations.

Kicki found her mother in the back yard hanging paper moon lanterns between the trees. Helping her was Gudrun, a young woman everyone thought would one day marry Kicki's oldest brother, and tonight Kicki was sure of it, for hadn't he invited Gudrun to join his family for the *Kräft-premiär?* When Kicki was satisfied that Mama and Gudrun had sufficiently "oohed" and "ahed" over her catch, she ran for the house.

"Don't touch the melon or the red raspberries! They're for afterwards," her mother called to her.

Kicki found her grandmother dropping fresh dill into a bubbling cauldron. When the old woman dumped the bucket of *kräftor* into the boiling water, Kicki smiled proudly. In days to come, the *kräftor* would be cooled in the same water they cooked in, then chilled to marinate at least twenty-four hours. But all across Sweden tonight was the premiere, so who could wait that long?

Thus it was only a few hours later, under the trees and paper lanterns, in the soft glow of the northern summer's lingering twilight, that Kicki handed out the songbooks to friends and family gathered round in their party hats. Tonight would be a night of singing and eating and merriment, of carefully peeling shellfish with special knives, of loudly sucking the heads for juicy yellow fat.

As Father poured glasses of potent aquavit for the grown-ups, Kicki looked at the big platter of *kräftor* she'd helped her grandmother carefully arrange and decorate with dill crowns and beside it the wheel of *kryddost* cheese and toasted bits of bread to eat the *kräft* tails on. Father complained there were less and less *kräftor* every year, but trying to decide which *kräft* she'd choose first, Kicki sighed at the size of the pile. How could there be so many crawfish in the world?

Swede enjoying Crayfish Premiere. Courtesy of Swedish Institute. Photo: Lennart Säät.

Crawfish Lexicon

EUROPEAN TONGUES

French	écrevisse
Gaelic	giomach-visge
German	flusskrebse
Hungarian	rák
Italian	gambero di fiume
Polish	raki
Portuguese	camerao-de-agua-doce
Romanian	creifis
Russian	pak
Spanish	ch'ol, cangrejo del rio
Swedish	kräftor
Turkish	kerevit su bocegi

NATIVE AMERICAN TONGUES

Biloxi	xonniyohi
Choctaw	shatje, shakchi
Cuicateco	sango yayicu
Cree	asakew
Lenape (Delaware)	schahamuis
Nahuatl	acocil, acocilin
Ofo	asho'hi
Totontepec	chacal
Yakima	k'astila

LANGUAGES OF THE PACIFIC RIM

Australian Aranda	iltjanma
Australian English	crayfish, yabby*
Australian Euahlayi	inga
Chinese	wah war hen
Maori	keewai, kooura
Japanese	zarigani, ebigani

*"Yabby" refers to both a specific species and to crawfish in general and is probably derived from "yaabitch," one of at least twenty-seven aboriginal words for crawfish.

Actually, her father was right. The quantity of crawfish that so impressed little Kicki was but a shadow of the bounty that once had been. Before the 1900s crawfish had been so plentiful in the lakes and rivers of Sweden that authorities saw no need for a closed season. With no season, obviously there was no season premiere, no end-of-summer ritual to celebrate the crawfish. But that doesn't mean they weren't enjoyed.

Before Columbus discovered America, as Europe pulled itself out of the Dark Ages and into the Renaissance, a multitude of princes, grand and petty alike, still called themselves the Holy Roman Empire. Gracing the feasts of many of those princes, and surely as well the rude tables of peasants bold enough to poach them, were crawfish. Away from the sea coast, the only tasty shellfish available is crawfish. Classed as seafood, not as meat, crawfish could be eaten even during the fasts the Catholic Church prescribed for at least one day each week and during the whole Lenten season. One can imagine the residents of some castle on the Rhine aflutter in preparations for the reigning prince's coming departure for the Holy Land to crusade against the Saracen. The highlight of his farewell banquet might be crawfish, caught in the river the week before and fed well so they would be fat for the evening's repast.

In Austria and Hungary, Hapsburg emperors prized intricately cooked crawfish so highly that they imposed strict regulations on the fishery. Minimum sizes were branded onto fishermen's oars to remove any excuse for noncompliance, but even exorbitant fines were never completely successful. Outlaws carried on a lively trade smuggling live crawfish north into Bavaria and south over the Alps for sale to Italian merchant princes.

Just as today we have feedlots for cattle, under the Salzburg archbishops monks devised elaborate systems for fattening up the crawfish. According to Reinhard Spitzy, an Austrian crawfish historian, "Before being cooked the poor animals had their middle tail-fin and so their intestine pulled out after having made them walk in cream and Schnapps."

In England, crawfish are mentioned in literary works, religious texts, and even household account books recording their purchase as early as the 1400s. In Shakespeare's time, according to Holinshed's Chronical, there were "little crafishes . . . taken . . . plentifullie in . . . fresh rivers." And if the Bard of Avon himself never wrote sonnets to praise them, as early as 1430 other poets did.

Queen Elizabeth I was treated to crawfish during a 1575 visit to Killingworth Castle, and in 1585 that old sea dog Sir Walter Raleigh received reports about crawfish in America. Most people have heard the story of how Sir Walter once laid his cape across a mud puddle so that Good Queen Bess would not get her slippers wet. Could his gambit with the cape really have been a clever ploy to get a monopoly on the American crawfish trade? Almost certainly not! But it's a fun thought.

As the British sailed out to claim an empire, they found the Indians of America and the aborigines of Australia enjoying crawfish as well. Apparently English colonists soon joined them at the table, for in 1606 Captain John Smith happily reported the presence in Virginia of "great craw-fishes . . . they have been taken in great quantities." And in Australia's early days as a penal colony, according to historian Robert Hughes, a convict might be lashed for "having a crayfish in his possession without authorization." Eventually, and inexplicably, the love of crawfish died out in England. In 1880 T. H. Huxley reported that they were seldom eaten there. One wonders why, for in so many other ways the British seem a clever people.

Of course, Spain was first to claim the New World, and to that royal court came back reports of lands "full of . . . crefysshes." Some of the treasure stolen from Mexico and Peru was certainly used to splurge on crawfish, priced at twenty-five centimos a hundred through most of the 1700s in the fish markets of the mother country. And if love of crawfish faded in England, in Spain the mudbugs held on with both pincers. In the twentieth century, American chroniclers of Iberia Ernest Hemingway and James Michener both pause in their literary musings to praise the crawfish they savored in the open-air restaurants of Spain.

The medieval French loved crawfish so much they even sewed their images into tapestries. Nowadays a more common expression of that amour is the endless spectrum of crawfish dishes, including (what most Americans would consider extraordinarily named) the *écrevisse à l'américaine*, in which the crawfish are doused with brandy and set aflame! Napoleon is known to have had his personal chef prepare crawfish to celebrate a battlefield victory, but it was after Waterloo that the popularity of *écrevisses* really surged in France, becoming by the mid-nineteenth century a fad of major proportions. Even with importation from Baltic countries and pond-raising to supplement the wild catch, supply could not meet demand. Imports from Finland alone went from 2 to 3 million crawfish a year in the 1860s to over 15 million at the turn of the century.

Prices rose, but high cost only made crawfish more chic. At the end of the nineteenth century, as America enjoyed the Gay

Nineteies, the French savored *la Belle Epoque.* Conspicuous consumption was de rigueur for any who could afford it, and expensive crawfish offered the most glamorous consumption of all, a way to show off both one's wealth and one's elegance. French food historian Robert Courtine claims, "A woman takes pleasure in eating crawfish because she knows that she is graceful."

But according to Courtine's American colleague Waverly Root, an invitation to eat crawfish also implied a man's desire to seduce, and acceptance indicated a woman's openness to such amorous liaisons. "A young lady invited to dine out, if she was ushered into one of those private restaurant dining rooms so popular at the period, remarkable for the tact and discretion of their staffs, to find a bucket of champagne and a bowl of crawfish on the table, knew what she had to expect." How could she not? Imagine your own self in one of those elegant rooms, closed to prying eyes, enjoying the sensuous repast. Piece by fragile piece, delicately the shell is peeled away, revealing the tender morsel that hides there. A tentative tongue snakes into the head to capture the succulent yellow tidbit within. Music and laughter steal through the doorway but do not distract, for your gaze belongs to the intoxicating person before you. You watch as your lover, one appetite sated, another coming to the fore, slowly bathes away crawfish nectar mingled with champagne, one finger at a time.

Courtine says, "Crayfish, in those days, were inseparable from lover's feasts. Young clerks dreamed of them, shopgirls who couldn't say no murmured yes to them in advance, and mashers revived their sated appetites with them." Ah, the French!

In the nineteenth century, the Industrial Revolution resulted in unprecedented factory pollution, which was largely dumped untreated into streams. Rivers were straightened, canals dug. Rising living standards meant more efficient sewerage disposal (also dumped untreated) and more food grown (adding fertilizer runoff to the problem). Long before the term "acid rain" appeared, drifting plumes of coal ash were poisoning waterways. Populations of aquatic creatures diminished or completely disappeared. Notably sensitive to water quality, crawfish became rarer. Diminishing stocks were protected by further restrictions or outright bans on catching them, but higher prices made illicit fishing all the more lucrative.

In 1860s France, the Marquis de Selve turned to raising crawfish in cultured ponds where numbers and growth could be controlled scientifically and there was protection from the deteriorating natural environment. Soon 12 million crawfish a year were leaving his ponds for the restaurants and fish markets of Paris. Still demand could not be met. Supplies in the wild kept shrinking. What *may* have happened next (no one's really sure) is that some anonymous conservationist's solution turned out to be a death blow. American crawfish were probably imported into Italy around 1860. That same creature had been totem to many of the American Indian tribes decimated three centuries before by European diseases, and in turn the American crawfish may be to blame for annihilating European crawfish.

Aphanomyces ataci is a fungus carried by some American crawfish. Immunity developed over the ages has rendered it a minor nuisance here, a sort of mudbug athlete's foot. But just as a conquistador's common cold became the American Indian's plague, so the American crawfish fungus was lethal to European species. The "plague" killed the crawfish that contracted it, then cast long-living spores into the water to seek other hosts. Spreading northward, it crossed the Alps into France in the 1870s, then hit Germany in 1877 and Austria in the 1880s. Streams became clogged with aquatic weeds and frog populations soared without crawfish to keep them in check. The plague continued northward. By the 1890s it had reached Poland, Lithuania, Estonia, Hungary, Russia and Finland.

Attempts to combat the disease began immediately, with renewed efforts continent-wide after the First World War. Reintroducing the native noble crawfish resulted in little success. Turkish crawfish were tried, but as their numbers grew, they too succumbed to the plague. Crawfish from the American East Coast were introduced, but their flavor was considered unacceptable.

Of course, Mother Nature is rarely completely thorough. The plague reduced the numbers of noble crawfish but did not render them extinct. In subsequent years the plague would return periodically in what scientists call epizootics, waves of death that occur whenever populations start to rebuild themselves. The pattern noted in Lithuania is typical: outbreaks in 1886, 1892, 1902, 1920, 1946, 1957, and 1963. To protect remaining stocks, authorities placed ever-stricter regulations on crawfishing. Shorter seasons were decreed and minimum sizes lowered to nine centimeters in France and eleven centimeters in Lithuania, a country that allows a fisherman only three traps and strictly outlaws hand fishing. In Poland, only male crawfish can be kept.

Cajun boys might feel sympathy for their counterparts near St. Petersburg. For the Louisianans, illegal "lamping" of rabbits is a rite of manhood. For the Russians, night crawfishing by torch light is likewise against the law. Even in the midst of such restrictions, however, the Soviet Union under Stalin in its drive to industrialize and collectivize agriculture pursued research to develop mechanical crawfish harvesters for an annual catch measured in the hundreds of tons. Russians loved crawfish long before Lenin. In his 1862 novel, *Fathers and Sons,* Ivan Turgenev has his characters send out for crawfish to impress a visiting cleric. The creatures make frequent appearances in Slavic folktales, riddles and proverbs. And as we saw earlier, Russian sexual slang includes the term "crawfish" to describe what Americans call the missionary position.

Under the commissars, workers continued to enjoy mudbugs. Bolshevik crawfish (which appropriately turned red when cooked) were usually purged a day or two in clear running water, dried four to six hours, then carefully packed in special wicker baskets for shipment. In summer, while rank and file comrades suffered in un-air-conditioned trains, crawfish traveled in refrigerator cars. In the 1960s, a brewmaster was publicly tried and imprisoned for watering down Zhiguli, a beer that proclaimed itself to be best to serve with crawfish in advertisements that showed a giant mudbug perched upon a keg holding in its claw an overflowing mug. At the close of the Communist era, crawfish were sold from aquarium-like tanks in Moscow shops for the state-controlled price of ten kopecks each.

The crawfish plague reached Sweden in 1907, where annual exports immediately dropped from ninety tons a year to thirty tons. Eventually the annual catch was only five percent of what it had been. Ironically, as catches decreased, the rituals surrounding crawfish grew. In Sweden, for children like little Kicki and adults as well, the opening of *kräft* season assumed the proportions of a national holiday, complete with New Year's Eve-style party hats (and hangovers). In Finland, Norway and Denmark, crawfish-eating

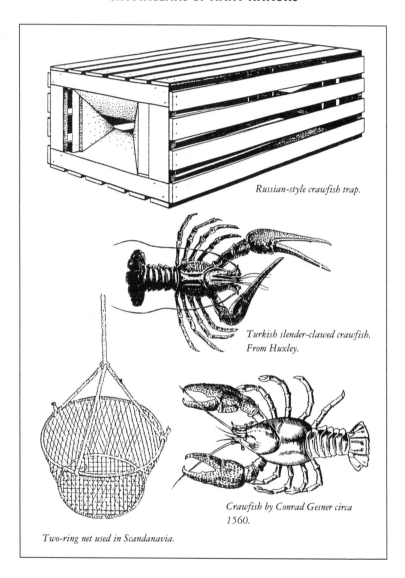

Russian-style crawfish trap.

Turkish slender-clawed crawfish.
From Huxley.

Crawfish by Conrad Gesner circa
1560.

Two-ring net used in Scandanavia.

Crawfish packaged for Swedish consumers. Courtesy of Breaux Bridge Export.

became the ritual that meant good-bye to summer. As turkey is associated with Thanksgiving in America, crawfish became a seasonal food in those places and remained so long after imports offered year-round supplies.

Soon Sweden was importing crawfish from the rest of Scandinavia and from Poland and the Soviet Union, but stocks were declining in those countries as well. Less flavorful slender-clawed crawfish were brought in from Rumania and Turkey, then others from America. In 1969 Swedes began restocking with signal crawfish taken from

Lake Tahoe in California, a species well suited both to the cold, clear Swedish waters and to the discriminating Swedish palate. At first, complains Austrian Reinhard Spitzy, Swedes kept the signal crawfish "as secret as the Coca-Cola company keeps their recipe," but eventually the Swedes reversed policy and became the signal crawfish nursery for the rest of Europe.

Crawfish aquaculture in Europe is largely limited to raising' hatchlings for release in the wild. Full-scale cultivation, in the words of one Frenchman, offers more "risques" than "bisques." By the late twentieth century the "Greens" political parties, expressing environmental concerns, were helping form a consensus to clean up the waters of Europe, certainly a step the crawfish would applaud with both claws. In 1978 what Dutch fishermen at first thought were Chinese shrimp turned out to be a species of crawfish long thought extinct. Perhaps there is yet room for optimism. On the southeast edge of the continent, Turkey, where crawfish are seldom eaten, became for a while the main supplier to western Europe. The lakes of Central Anatolia teemed with the creatures year-round, but after peaking in 1972, overfishing and pollution rapidly reduced the fishery.

South from Turkey, in Arabia there has never been much love lost on the crawfish, which was not only considered unclean, but in some quarters believed downright malevolent. There are reports of crawfish nailed to door posts to keep out evil spirits. According to Dr. James Avault, in Greece crawfish carcasses are hung in trees to dry up. After they die they became scarecrows "in vegetable gardens to protect against diseases."

Crawfish are only slightly more appreciated in East Africa, where the American red swamp species was introduced in the 1960s and

1970s. They are eaten in Uganda, but Kenyans blame local lack of interest on the expense of traps and the fact that mudbugs look too much like bugs. An effort to export to Sweden failed, blamed on primitive infrastructure and local resistance to licensing foreign dealers.

The crawfish may have been introduced to East African lakes to eat snails that carry human diseases. The same species was imported into Japan in the 1930s, not to feed humans but to feed bullfrogs brought in three decades earlier. Soon there were more crawfish than frogs, however. The Japanese turned their noses up at the idea of consuming American crawfish. One explanation is that the presence of a parasitic lung fluke makes crawfish unsuitable for being served raw; others claim that most Japanese are genetically incapable of digesting American crawfish. In either case, the huge concentrations of mudbugs have made great pests of themselves, clipping rice shoots and burrowing through levees. In the American South, where imported Japanese kudzu runs wild and imported Japanese water hyacinths clog the waters, the locals may perhaps be permitted a smile at their crawfish's Japanese predations.

In Japan, the red swamp crawfish joined the indigenous *cambaroides* species native as well to Korea, Manchuria and the Russian Far East, and from Japan, imported red swamp crawfish spread to China, wreaking havoc in rice paddies, carp ponds, and irrigation ditches, where farmers who spotted them would smash them like bugs. But it is said that in China everything is either eaten or used in medicine, and indeed some Chinese-Americans report their parents in inland Szechuan province using home-caught crawfish in recipes calling for shrimp. By the 1990s, Chinese crawfish were being caught on a commercial scale, then processed for export.

In Australia, crawfish are called crayfish and sometimes lobsters. True saltwater lobsters are often called crawfish. It's not that things are backward down under, it's just that that's the way the language shook out when the English arrived to find so many unfamiliar species needing names. If it seems odd to call crawfish lobsters, bear in mind that one crawfish species on the island of Tasmania regularly reaches seven and a half pounds, and some have been reported to reach thirteen pounds! Even on the mainland, an adult "Murray River lobster" (again, a freshwater crawfish) weighs in at a healthy five and a half pounds.

More recognizable to Americans and Europeans would be the marrons of southwest Australia (named by a French immigrant who thought they tasted sweet as *marrons,* chestnuts), the Sydney crayfish of the southeast, and the ubiquitous yabby, sometimes called a nipper. Australians have a love-hate relationship with yabbies, praising their flavor and making fun of their habits but decrying their "dambusting" burrowing. Ranging across and beyond the southeastern quadrant of the continent, yabbies inhabit the most lifeless-seeming desert to the fringe of the rain forest, and in rivers, lakes, ditches, ponds and the seasonally dry creek beds Australians call *billabongs,* where they've been known to stay burrowed for up to eight years waiting for the next rain.

Like crawfish the world over, they feed a host of predators—fish, birds, turtles and people, who not only eat them but prize them for bait. Other than a prohibition on taking females "in berry" (carrying eggs) there are no size or bag limits and it's open season year-round. Though there is keen interest in aquaculture, as of the late 1980s experimental farming had been largely unsuccessful (though farmers in northern Australia meet much success with the tropical redclaw crayfish).

Active in summer, during the rainy season yabbies will often migrate en masse with what some say is a supernatural ability to seek out the farmer's pond where they can do the most damage. Paranoid theories aside, it is true that young yabbies do have the rather extraordinary ability to clump together into a ball in order to survive a river's turbulent currents. When they reach calmer water, they let go of one another and continue on their merry way.

Archaeologists have found fossil records of yabbies eaten by aboriginal Australians at least 28,000 years ago, the oldest hard evidence (no pun intended) of crawfish consumption to date. In modern times, the image of children yabbying in a roadside ditch with a baited piece of string is such a national folk icon that it appears in books, movies, and even on postage stamps. In the words of one writer, "The yabby has a high profile in Australian folklore."

But if they serve as a cultural symbol down under, nowhere in the world are crawfish so enmeshed in the ethnic psyche as among the Cajuns of Louisiana.

CRAWFISH-CRAVING CAJUNS

AW, come on, Margaret. Look at all that food. You'd never know there was a war on."

Margaret Braswell just wasn't sure she could bring herself to eat those little things. Growing up in the red clay hills of Arcadia, Louisiana, best known as the place where Bonnie and Clyde met their end, she'd been familiar with crawfish since childhood when she and friends would use a piece of bacon to lure the critters from their holes. But that was just mischief to fill idle moments. There in the heart of Anglo-north Louisiana no civilized person would have ever considered *eating* crawfish.

But Margaret no longer lived in Arcadia. Now a school teacher in south Louisiana, she found herself courted by dark and dashing LeRoy Benoit, and today come a-visiting were LeRoy's sister, Mae, and her husband whose bald head had earned him the nickname

"Shine." With them they'd brought a tub of crawfish which just now had been pulled red and steaming from the boiling water. World War II was raging in the Pacific. In Europe, Hitler was still winning. At home, gasoline was rationed. Meat was rationed, and flour, and cooking oil, and sugar. Everything was rationed, it seemed, but no one had bothered to ration crawfish, and war or not, her beau's Cajun relations were determined to throw a feast in her honor.

LeRoy found Margaret in the kitchen, huddled over the sink with the plate of crawfish he had carefully peeled for her. "Everybody's wondering what happened to you," he said in the accent she found so strange and intriguing.

"I'll be with you soon," she answered, a defiant cast to her chin as she moved aside to let LeRoy see what she was doing. One by one she was washing the peeled crawfish tails, then one by one she was drying them on a dishcloth, with the methodical precision that would one day make her a good librarian. If she was going to eat these things, she was going to make sure they were clean.

Margaret risked a glance at LeRoy and found him smiling. It was a compromise both could live with—the first of many, for eventually Margaret married LeRoy and bore him four children. Growing up in Lake Charles, Louisiana, those children would all eat crawfish, and by adulthood at least would not even consider being ashamed of it. But things had not always been that way, even well south of Margaret's hometown of Arcadia.

The story starts in another place called Arcadia but spelled in the French fashion, Acadie. There on the Bay of Fundy in what is now Nova Scotia, Canada, the kingdom of France first established a toehold in North America. Eventually Acadians reclaimed tidal marshlands, built farms and prospered. Geo-politics proved their down-fall, for their tiny colony formed a strategic pivot between New France to the north and New England to the south. England captured Acadie and in 1755, its governor decided to deport the Acadians. Deporting an entire population is no easy job. Some Acadians escaped to the woods and others became guerrilla fighters, but most were loaded onto ships, young men first, then old men and boys, women and children. Families were torn apart, some never to reunite.

In his poem *Evangeline,* Longfellow chronicles their hardships, but Longfellow omitted some other sufferers. In the waters of the harbor were lobsters who, it is said, were very sad over the Acadians' forced departure—so sad, in fact, that the lobsters determined to follow the Acadians into exile. Alas, the road was not a straight one. The British planned to divvy up the exiles among the thirteen American colonies where they'd be sold as indentured servants to cover the cost of transporting them. But some colonies wouldn't let the Acadians land. Other enacted harsh restrictions. In Philadelphia, the "City of Brotherly Love," Acadian children were taken away to be placed with English-speaking families.

The Acadians' first impulse was to escape. Overland they crossed the Appalachians, looking for French territory. In open boats they tried to sail back to Acadie. One exile, Beausoleil Broussard, led a mutiny that captured the ship transporting them! But more often, Acadians wound up in the West Indies, where they died by the hundreds of tropical fevers, or in England, where they languished in concentration camps. Through all this, the lobsters were following, crawling along the ocean bottom. (At least the Acadians were in ships.) Weary though they became, the lobsters did not give up. It was a stubbornness for which their descendants would be legendary.

In the 1760s word spread that a New Acadia was being founded in *Louisiane,* which at the time belonged to Spain but was populated mostly by French-speakers. Over the next two decades, Acadians from around the world headed for Louisiana to reunite with kin or at least put an end to traveling.

But if the Acadians were tired of traveling, imagine how the lobsters felt. Their journey had been so long and so hard that each time they molted, instead of getting bigger, they got smaller—and smaller, and smaller, and smaller. When finally they crawled into the bayous, they'd grown so small they weren't lobsters at all anymore.

And that, any Cajun grandmother will tell you, is how there came to be crawfish in south Louisiana.

Of course, that crawfish tale doesn't explain how mudbugs had found their way into the cuisine of New Orleans as early as its founding in 1718. An early source reports crawfishing with frog legs for bait. More likely it was frog carcasses after the big hind legs were removed for human consumption. (The appetite of the French for frog legs was well known; this fondness gave rise to a common ethnic slur, and also, since the French word for frog is *crapaud,* led to the American name for a French game of dice, "craps.") A visitor to Cajun country in 1900 noted garden ponds for keeping crawfish. Probably these *platins,* a natural feature of the Louisiana prairie that may mark ancient buffalo wallows, also watered crops and livestock and provided paddies for casually cultivated "Providence rice" as well as mud to mix with Spanish moss for the *bousillage* that plastered walls and chimneys.

As all those activities attest, Cajuns were well settled in Louisiana by the beginning of the twentieth century and were absorbing other immigrant groups who found their fun-loving ways attractive. But as parents so often preach to teenage daughters, being considered "fun" is not necessarily being respected.

"Cribisse! Cribisse!," a folk song common in both English and French-Creole versions at least through the 1930s when it was collected by Irène Whitfield, was often sung by African-American children to tease their Cajun contemporaries:

> Poor crawfish ain't got no show,
> Frenchmen catch them and make gumbo.
> Go all around the Frenchman's beds,
> Don't find nothing but crawfish heads.
> Frenchman! Frenchman! Nine days old!
> Broke his hand in a crawfish hole.

Not very respectful of crawfish, nor of the people who eat them! Both the children taunting and those taunted would have been amazed to hear that a half-century later Cajun food would sweep the nation. In those days, "Cajun" implied someone quaintly provincial at best and primitive and uneducable at worst. In the Jim Crow segregated south, anyone openly scorned by blacks surely rested on the bottom rung of society's ladder.

In 1982, Samuel Eyner celebrated the seventy-five years he had spent in Louisiana after one of the famous "orphan trains" took him from a home for foundlings in New York City and dropped him off, linguistically stranded, with a French-speaking family on Louisiana's lower Red River. "I was born Yankee. I grew up

Creole, because Cajun was low-class. Nowadays I guess I'm Cajun."

If Cajuns were low-class, to the Anglo-American majority craw-fish were even lower class, a food of hungry hillbillies and swamp-ers. As late as 1953, a New Orleans electric company entitled one of its periodic pamphlets for homemakers "Crayfish Eradication." Even Sydney Guidry of Catahoula, who became wealthy in the crawfish business, shrugs apologetically when he explains why his family ate them when he was a boy. "We had to do something. They were bit-ing our toes."

Fearing the twin dangers of a militant linguistic minority and a permanent underclass, as early as the 1920s Louisiana's educational establishment invoked systematic efforts to wipe out the use of French in Louisiana, just as authorities in France were attacking Breton, and the Germans Wendish, and the English Gaelic.

Low-class or not, Cajuns and crawfish were already inseparably linked. Another verse of "Cribisse! Cribisse!" runs:

> Crawfish ain't scared of a six-mule team,
> But run from a Frenchman every time he see him.

The same motifs—brave crawfish and Cajuns with hearty, all-inclusive appetites—still appeared in a variety of tall tales into the 1990s, but by then Cajuns were telling the jokes themselves, witness to the great shift since the 1930s in the status of Cajuns and crawfish alike. On a 1930s recording, regional comic Walter Coquille in his persona of "the mayor of Bayou Pom Pom" avowed, "I always stand up for the crawfish because he is the symbol of the Bayou Pom Pom." Maintaining that the mudbug is braver than the national symbol, the eagle, the mayor offered the following proof: "Put the eagle on a railroad track. Let that train come along, blow that horn, ring that bell. That eagle will fly away. Ah, but put the crawfish on the track. He will raise his hands to stop that train. He would rather die than move."

No matter how limitless its bravery, the crawfish's main relationship to Cajuns had always been one of consumed to consumer, and it was just that connection that made crawfish a symbol of Cajuns to the nation at large. Like Elvis after him, in the late 1940s Hank Williams helped launch his career on Shreveport's "Louisiana Hayride" radio show. Fellow musician Dudley Bernard recalls that while touring dance halls in the southern part of that state, Williams was looking for a song that would capture Cajun lifestyle. "I told him, 'If you tell me what you're looking for, Hank, I'll write it for you.' He said, 'If I knew what I was looking for, I'd write it myself.' Well, he did." The result was the national hit "Jambalaya." No matter that many claim Williams lifted the melody from "Grand Texas," a jaunty Cajun lament about a wife running off. The lyrics were his, and the song's refrain of "Jambalaya, crawfish pie, filé gumbo" celebrated all that was delightfully exotic about Cajun cuisine.

A few years later, when Johnny Horton's "North to Alaska" soared up the charts, Cajun artist Johnnie Allan made a 1962 regional hit rewriting it as "South to Louisiana." Instead of rushing north to hunt for gold, Allan's Cajuns were paddling to Thibodaux where "The crawfish are biting, the girls are exciting."

The very next year Clovis Clemence emerged from his mud chimney and into children's literature in the book *Clovis Crawfish and His Friends.* Over the next thirty years author Mary Alice Fontenot would add ten books to the hugely popular series, each with a sprinkling of French words and a Cajun children's song.

Many of the stories reflect contemporary south Louisiana life (such as the oil patch Texan influx represented by a clumsy but friendly armadillo) or borrow from native fold traditions. When Clovis fills a molted cricket's empty shell with mud, attaching leaves as wings to fool a blue jay, he borrows from tricksters such as Brer Rabbit or French Louisiana's Bouki and Lapin.

With books offering such innocuous morals as "cooperation is good," it's easy to forget what bold, even radical pioneers Clovis and author Fontenot were. In 1962 when the series premiered, Cajun children were still being punished for speaking French on school grounds. Yet these books actually promoted French for children: "'It was a big bétail,' which is the way to say 'a big animal' in south Louisiana." Not *a* way to say it, *the* way to say it. Here was slick propaganda promoting an ethnic revival, all the more subversive for its being in a sweet, child-enticing package. Like Walter Coquille's crawfish on the railroad track, Clovis was raising his claws to fight a half-century of institutionalized efforts to eradicate French in Louisiana. By 1968, le Conseil pour le Développement du Français en Louisiane (CODOFIL) was importing teachers from France, Belgium and Quebec to bolster Louisiana French, much as American crawfish reseeded Europe's depleted lakes and streams.

In the 1970s, another series featured a fisherman whose incantation, "Spanish moss in my hand, turn me into Crawfish-man," rendered him a "super-hereaux." Through five paperback adventures, Tim Edler's Crawfish-man fought enemies based on villains in fairy tales (an evil witch), popular movies (*Star Wars*-inspired Dark Gator) and even the politics of the Cajun Renaissance. When CODOFIL panned one book, the next featured a bumbling henchman named Kodofeel. In one tale, Crawfish-man rescues Ron Guidry,

Children's book character, Crawfish-man. Courtesy of Tim Edler, Little Cajun Books.

a Cajun baseball pitcher whose 1978 25-3 season for the New York
Yankees won him the Cy Young award. In another, he recommends
summertime activities for kids. Mixed in with cock fights and
chewing sugarcane are crawfishing, going to a crawfish boil and
peeling crawfish! While a super-hereaux may feel safe, such ideas
probably made Clovis turn over in his chimney, but the suggestions
were signs of their times. By the 1980s crawfish were everywhere
and as a symbol had become inseparable from Cajuns who suddenly
found themselves "cool."

Of course Cajuns were not alone in their surging pride. Around
the country, ethnic group after ethnic group knocked dents in the

melting pot. A Bayou Lafourche levee inspector recalls, "That TV show 'Roots' opened the door and crawfish backed right in." Many of them backed into boiling pots at south Louisiana *bouillitures,* events centered around eating large quantities of shrimp, crabs and crawfish. According to Professor Jay Huner, Director of the University of Southwestern Louisiana's Crawfish Research Center, "Crawfish boils are important social gatherings . . . comparable in every way to New England clam bakes and southwest barbecues."

When the 1980s oil glut economy sent many Cajuns once more into exile, this time the crawfish followed them by air freight. For alumni of Louisiana State University, University of Southwestern Louisiana, and other schools, crawfish boils featuring flown-in mudbugs became rallying points from San Diego to Maine.

As chefs nationwide discovered Cajun cuisine (or approximations of it) crawfish burrowed into menus from Manhattan to Los Angeles. National approval reinforced their status as Cajun symbol. Several Louisiana makers of *boudin* began replacing pork with crawfish in the sausage's recipe. Regional brand Zapp's Potato Chips came out with a peppery "Cajun Craw-tater" flavor. It soon became almost mandatory for Louisianans visiting out of state to take along some crawfish.

Allan "Sprinky" Durand, co-producer of the 1986 motion picture *Belizaire the Cajun,* remembers how, when the movie was still a pipe dream, he was invited to the Sundance Institute in Utah, founded by Robert Redford to give promising filmmakers a helping hand. "I wasn't too confident about my filmmaking abilities, but I knew how to cook crawfish," Sprinky says, so he brought along several ice chests with enough étouffée for the seventy or so institute guests. "There we were, me and the director, serving étouffée to Sydney

Pollock, Robert Duvall, and the 'Big Red One' [Redford] himself. Not only did I get invited back, but we got the movie made, and I'll go to my grave believing it was 'cause of the crawfish."

It had been three decades since Elvis sang, "I pulled Mr. Crawfish out of his hole," to open the movie *King Creole,* based on an early novel by Harold Robbins. Now not only did *Belizaire* have an obligatory crawfish-eating scene, but musical groups like the Radiators and Bonedaddys were recording mudbug anthems. Pioneer rocker and Rock and Roll Hall of Fame inductee Professor Longhair titled a 1980 album "Crawfish Fiesta." And in 1991, tens of thousands of music fans roared their approval when, as the last act of the day, Cajun rocker Zachary Richard took the main stage at the New Orleans Jazz and Heritage Festival costumed as a crawfish.

While their slow forward motion and habit of scurrying backward have made crawfish an inappropriate symbol for sports teams, the name does adorn a group of baton-twirlers, the Ecrevettes, and in tennis, where even top players do a lot of backing up to cover the court, crawfish-handled rackets graced sweatshirts in the 1988 Virginia Slims Tennis Tournament in New Orleans. Soon all the grass-roots activity forced legislative action. In 1983, by Act No. 572 of the state legislature, the crawfish became the state crustacean, joining a pantheon of symbols that includes the pelican, the magnolia, the bald cypress, and the official state dog, the Catahoula cur.

Crawfish were everywhere. Driving into Lafayette, the "Hub of Acadiana," a visitor sees artsy stylized crawfish, photo-realist crawfish, cuddly cartoon crawfish and some that defy description plastered on billboards promoting hotels, restaurants and tourist attractions. If Hilton Hotels are "America's business address," at the

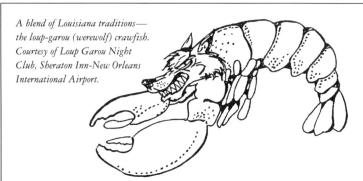

A blend of Louisiana traditions—the loup-garou (werewolf) crawfish. Courtesy of Loup Garou Night Club, Sheraton Inn-New Orleans International Airport.

Crawfish-theme lottery game. Courtesy of Louisiana Lottery Commission.

Lafayette Hilton crawfish are an inextricable part of the business. In the hotel restaurant, not only do crawfish appear in virtually all the house specialties, they can also serve as your appetizer, garnish your salad, or top your steak. In the gift shop, in addition to the mandatory crawfish books, tee shirts and key chains, one can also buy crawfish beer can insulators, crawfish-shaped paddle balls, taxidermied crawfish magnets, and more. Another hotel, the Sheraton Inn at New Orleans International Airport, dedicated its nightclub to the loup-garou, "the Cajun-French legend of the werewolf or ghost crawfish." It was what folklorists call fakelore, but what the public calls fun.

Dozens of craftspeople began incorporating crawfish designs (if not the crawfish themselves) into jewelry, souvenir kitsch and folk art. One graphic artist designed a Louisiana alphabet poster with the letters formed of crawdads, while another published a book of cartoons, *101 Uses for a Louisiana Crawfish*. The New Orleans Mudbug Company began making sculptures (what else can you call them?) of taxidermied crawfish posed in boxing rings, on surfboards, even feasting at a table of boiled people! By 1990, the mail order Louisiana Catalog could offer crawfish-shaped cookie jars, neckties, earrings, rubber stamps, letter openers, coffee mugs, even wicker baskets. Crawfish-decorated drygoods could cover you from head (your choice of cap or kerchief) to toe (crawfish shoelaces).

The souvenir tee shirt offered a ready canvas upon which crawfish might crawl. While many tees merely feature piles of boiled crawfish, designs that anthropomorphize, that is, imbue mudbugs with human characteristics, often with a healthy dose of irony, seem more popular. They also chart social history. Snow-skiing crawfish in designer snowsuits preached "Ski Louisiana," a state that has

*"Nightmare on the Bayou," crawfish enjoying a feast of humans,
by New Orleans Mud Bug Company.*

neither mountains nor snow. "Hot Tubbing Louisiana Style"
showed crawfish actually enjoying being boiled, and no wonder,
with tuxedoed alligator waiters ready to cater to their every whim.

If such designs epitomized the free-spending 1980s, the 1990s
were ushered in with psychedelic "craw-dudes" and the local variant
of a national fad, "Mutant Ninja Crawfish."

Many souvenir tee shirts seek to titillate with the easily mis-
understood instructions for eating boiled crawfish. Out of context,
the words "Pinch me, Peel me, Eat me" or "Pinch the Tails and
Suck the Heads" seem rather suggestive emblazoned across one's

chest. One design shows a buxom brunette holding a crawfish and asking, "You want me to suck what?"

Perhaps the best measure of the popularity of cultural symbols from region to region is the frequency of appearance by the crawfish and the alligator on T-shirts. While some designs include both, showing them dancing or playing music together, usually only one or the other appears.

During her quarter-century in the souvenir business, Sandra Broussard of Lagniappe of New Orleans, Ltd., has witnessed the rise of crawfish (often actually lobsters with trimmed-down claws) as Cajun symbol on aprons, souvenir plates, collectible spoons, salt shakers and the other miscellany that is her stock-in-trade. The raccoon, once favored, has all but faded from use. "Now it's all crawfish and alligators," she explains, with their relative popularity being a good measure of an area's ethnic mix.

"In Shreveport, in north Louisiana, it's mostly alligators we sell. Even in New Orleans, the alligators edge out the crawfish. But in Lafayette, that's Cajun country, and crawfish just *eat* those alligators!"

HOW TO . . .

CATCHING CRAWFISH in many areas ranks up there with
berry picking as family fun. Its low tech requirements make it
available to anyone, no matter how young, no matter how poor.
Can't get out to the country? Ponds in your local city park might
well reward you with a feast.

People frequently catch crawfish by hand, either by reaching into
their burrows or plucking them off the ground. In rocky streams,
turning over stones will often uncover crawfish. (Maybe that's why
we say, "Leave no stone unturned"!)

The food-from-the-wild-expert Euell Gibbons described gathering crawfish by flashlight in a cornfield with his grandfather. This
author's father, Loulan Pitre, and aunt, Vesta Sueur, often recount
how as children on nights after a good rain they would pick crawfish off the ground in sugarcane fields.

Emelie and Hannah Callais inspect their catch. Photo: G. Pitre.

The New Zealand Maori baited bundles of ferns to catch craw-fish. Native Americans skewered venison on sharpened sticks that they drove into a creek bottom, pulling it out periodically to harvest the mudbugs clinging to the bait.

The technique of baited twine attached to a stick is still common in France, was used in Louisiana at least as early as 1753, and was probably *the* most common method of crawfishing all across America, if one can judge by the first line of "The Crawdad Song": "You get a line and I'll get a pole, Baby."

Early fishermen of the Atchafalaya Basin traded the pole for a float so they could tend several lines at once. Checking with a dip net, they hoped to avoid lamenting "the one that got away."

N E T S of one type or another have been used around the globe for catching crawfish. In Louisiana, foot-square lift nets stretched on two V-shaped wires may have been replaced by the trap for commercial crawfishing but still work fine for a Sunday afternoon with the kids. In Sweden, a *håv* (round lift net) gives way to the larger *mjärde* trap used by more serious fishermen. In nineteenth-century France, a hoop net baited with frogs was preferred.

Crawfish pots, like lobster pots with wooden slats, were occasionally used in Louisiana and were long common on the Baltic coast of the Russian Empire. The plastic crawfish pots (a lot like minnow traps) available in local sporting goods stores are still the favorite of Oregon's commercial crawfishery.

B A I T S in common use are ample proof that crawfish eat anything. Artificial baits (mostly compressed grain and fishmeal) readily available in Louisiana usually only supplement fish. Roadside crawfishermen prefer chicken necks or good, smelly "melt" (beef spleen). Across south Louisiana, as much as budding trees or blooming wildflowers signal spring, so do "Melt for Sale" signs placed in supermarket windows.

On the West Coast, pierced cans of dog food are a popular bait. To keep costs down, many professionals in Oregon's Willamette Valley use cheaper dry dog food to bait their pots.

T O F I S H W I T H O U T B A I T other methods bear mention. In his 1880 book, T. H. Huxley described "fires lighted on the banks at night, and the crayfish, which are attracted, like moths, to the unwonted illumination, are scooped out with the hand or with nets."

If a creek lacks good cover, empty tin cans attract crawfish looking for a place to hide. The cans make them easy to pick up, too. In 1789 a German encyclopedia gave detailed instructions on how to catch crawfish with song, including the notes of a melody guaranteed to draw them "out of their hiding places and . . . to the music." Good luck.

WHEN TO GO CRAWFISHING depends on where you are and what the weather is. Crawfish are cold-blooded creatures (no insult intended) and so take their temperature from the surrounding water. If it's too cold, they are sluggish and slow to go after your bait (though Gary Florczak in Wisconsin claims much success crawfishing through a hole in the ice). When it's too hot, many species will burrow out of sight.

On the Gulf of Mexico, March through May is the best time, and in the Pacific Northwest, June through September. Appropriate judgments should be made for other areas.

PET CRAWFISH thrive in aquariums, where they tend to be hardier than many fin-fish. Not only are they fascinating while crawling around the tank, they do just fine spending short periods out of water, where they prove themselves mobile and fearless. Some people claim crawfish can even learn to recognize their masters, but I wouldn't count on it.

Two gallons of bottled water are about right for the average mudbug. An aerator pump is nice but not essential. Putting down a layer of gravel will help keep the tank clean. At meal times, little Clovis would enjoy a *live* insect, earthworm, or small goldfish. Of course, don't put but a crawfish in a tank with any precious fish, for the mudbug will eat them. Do not feed your crawfish more than two or three times a week. Overfeeding will kill them.

WHAT KIND OF CRAWFISH TO COOK will be determined largely by where you are. In the Pacific Northwest you'll find signal crawfish with their characteristic flared tails. In Wisconsin, the *virilis,* though growing scarce, are favored because *immunis* run small and rusties are hard to peel.

Along the Gulf and Atlantic coasts you'll generally see red swamp crawfish with a few white river crawfish mixed in. Despite their evocative names, the differences between them are subtle and need not concern you. Most purchased sacks will contain some of both.

In short, though gourmets may argue the relative merits of one species over another, when it comes to cooking, a crawfish is a crawfish is a crawfish, especially once the fat is removed.

BUYING CRAWFISH is more a matter of finding the best price. Though there are several proposals under discussion, as of 1992 there was no federal inspection of seafood comparable to the checks on meat and poultry. Fortunately, when you're trying to buy live crawfish there's an easy way to tell whether or not they will be fit to eat—if they're dead, don't buy them.

A live crawfish will snap at you when you approach it from the front, but chilled crawfish can get pretty sluggish, so don't be fooled. Pick up the crawfish from behind—go ahead, pinch it with thumb and index finger at about the middle of its body, it can't get you—and its tail should curl up.

Even when crawfish are crowded into a sack, you should be able to *hear* them. No offense to Kellogg but they make a snap, crackle, and pop sound.

If you decide to buy from a roadside vendor, does he have a shady spot? Crawfish kept too hot and too long in a crowded sack will pass through the pearly gates long before they reach your pearly whites. If you're in doubt, ask the vendor to open the sack for closer inspection. If he won't, keep your money in your pocket.

H O W   M U C H   T O   B U Y depends not only on how many but also on who you're serving. Will this be a novelty garnish or a main course for a pro who grew up on crawfish? Served Scandinavian style, eight to sixteen crawfish per person is about right. Many of your guests won't even get that far if you follow the traditional formula of a shot of 80-proof aquavit for every crawfish eaten. For Cajuns, five pounds per adult is usual, though caterers often allow only two and a half pounds.

If you're peeling them for another dish, remember that live crawfish yield about twelve to sixteen percent of their weight in cooked tail meat. So for each typical three and one-half ounces of tail meat that will flavor a single serving of étouffée, gumbo, etc., you'll need to peel one and a half pounds of crawfish. Of course in many stores you can buy already-peeled tail meat. A one-pound bag will make four healthy servings.

K E E P I N G   C R A W F I S H   A L I V E once you buy a sack is as important as checking them beforehand. Don't drop the sack. Keep it out of sunlight or a hot car trunk. Laying the sack on its side, not upright, puts less weight on the guys at the bottom. If you're lucky enough to have a lot of crawfish, don't stack sacks if you can help it.

Chilling (not freezing) the crawdads will do much to prolong their longevity. At thirty-eight degrees crawfish will survive several days in the sack. *Don't* wash them or hose them down until you're ready to cook them, unless you have a source of pure water. The chlorine found in most drinking water may hurt them.

B U Y I N G   C O O K E D   C R A W F I S H , requires you to check temperature, smell, and the curl of the tail. Unless they're fresh out

Backyard cooking rig. Photo: G. Pitre.

of the pot, whole boiled crawfish should be stored colder than forty degrees. You'll probably whiff spices as well as the seafood-y scent of cooked shellfish, but if they smell *bad,* they are. Crawfish boiled live usually have their tails curled up under them. Crawfish boiled dead have straight tails, mushy meat and bad flavor. Toss them out.

P R E P A R A T I O N   F O R   B O I L I N G includes washing the crawfish, usually in a foot tub. When you're dealing with a sack full, typically forty pounds, this is a job best done outside. Dump the crawfish into the tub and fill it almost full with water. After ten minutes, drain.

Many people repeat this step with fresh water two or three times, but depending on the crawfish and your tastes, that may be unnecessary. Purging is essentially the same process but involves adding as much as a box of salt to the water. Though it is a common practice, purging is not recommended since it toughens the meat.

In many areas discount or sporting goods stores sell outdoor boiling rigs that are very practical if you cook up large quantities of shellfish (or anything else) more than once in a blue moon. A large kettle, usually aluminum, is fitted with a wire basket so that what you cook can be easily pulled out and drained without your having to dump the hot water you may want for the next batch. Connected to a small butane tank (refillable at any recreational vehicle dealership) is an adjustable gas burner that doubles as platform to support the kettle.

S P I C I N G   T H E   W A T E R is a matter of ethnic as well as individual taste. A Scandinavian cannot imagine crawfish without the taste of fresh dill. A Viennese may want his or hers boiled in beer. In America's Pacific Northwest, pickling spices are traditionally used and can be bought by the jar or mixed into a unique blend with cloves, mustard seeds and a host of other aromatic flavorings.

Cajuns have their own preferred spices. Typical additions to ten gallons of water would be one and one-half pounds of salt, three or four quartered lemons, three or four tablespoons of red pepper, and a few head of onions and garlic.

Other spices such as bay leaf and allspice, which are more Creole than Cajun in tradition, were often tied into a cheesecloth bouquet garni that could be removed after cooking. Commercial spice packets, commonly called "crab boil," have been around for decades. Liquid crab boil is stronger, cheaper and even more convenient, but some people complain that it imparts a medicinal flavor. Cooks often use a belt-and-suspenders approach and put in some of both. Others add a lump of sugar or dollop of honey, just for flavor.

Large commercial boilers often spice and salt crawfish *after* they are cooked, speculating that the spices will get on the diner's fingers and thus to the mouth. Though it is cost-effective, this method often results in burning lips and bland crawfish. Some folks swear by it. This author does not. Crawfish may also be steamed, just as one steams vegetables, to achieve the same effect as boiling.

BOILING TIME is important. Overcooked crawfish are hard to peel, and raw or grossly undercooked crawfish should never be eaten; they may carry flukes that can be dangerous. In 1553 the French writer Rabelais advised cooking crawfish till they're "as red as a cardinal's hat." It's still sound advice, but more specific instructions may be helpful.

Dump your crawfish into boiling water. When the water comes back to a boil, start timing. If you're in a hurry, boil for ten

Backyard crawfish boil. Photo: G. Pitre.

minutes, them immediately remove the crawfish from the hot
water. For maximum spiciness boil them only five minutes, turn off
the heat, and let the crawfish remain in the hot water for ten or
fifteen minutes more, or even longer, but periodically check one to
make sure they aren't overcooking.

Others prefer boiling them the full ten minutes, then shutting
the flame and dumping a bag of ice into the pot. The water cools
quickly, so cooking stops, and the crawfish can be left to soak up
flavor. Never put cooked crawfish back in the container that held
them when they were alive unless you thoroughly wash it first.

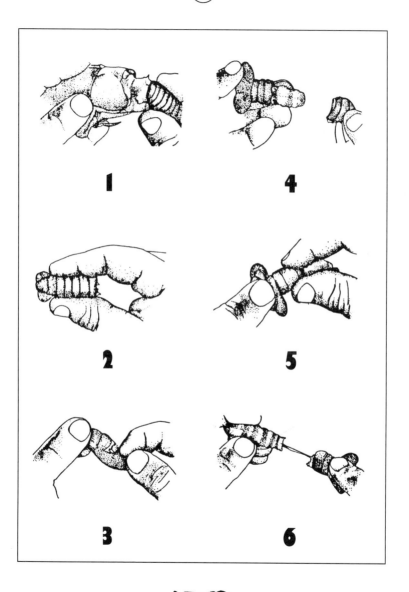

1

2

3

4

5

6

Do crawfish feel pain when you drop them in? To quote T. H. Huxley, "nothing short of being a crayfish would give us positive assurance." It should be remembered however that the nervous system of a crawfish is infinitely simpler than our own. They have no brain, only a thick ganglion at one end of the nerve cord. And boiling water brings death quickly.

S E R V I N G boiled crawfish, like cooking them, is often a matter of ethnic heritage. Scandinavians carefully arrange them with dill flowers. The French stack them into a pyramid called a *buisson d'écrevisses*. Americans are rarely so neat; Cajuns like to cover the table with newspaper and pour out a pile (to the occasional dismay of out-of-town guests who expected a formal dinner).

In Scandinavia, special crawfish knives allow adept Swedes to scoop meat from tail and claw with a dexterity that would impress any Cajun. To keep clean, they wear bibs and use place mats. Cajuns use their fingers and often employ wide, deep individual trays, which, like the Scandinavians' place mats, often have pictures of crawfish on them. In either case, keep lots of napkins handy, and remember that cloth towels are better for the planet than paper.

P E E L I N G is not much of a chore when crawfish have been properly cooked. Twist and pull the tail away from the head, then squeeze near the base of the tail (thumb underneath, index finger on top), bite down on the meat that extends past the tail shell, then pull the shell away. It's really that easy, and with a little practice you'll see how those big piles of crawfish go down so fast.

If the crawfish are overcooked, or if you're peeling to use them in another dish (and therefore don't want to use your teeth) peel off the first two or three segments of the shell at the top of the tail to give yourself a better grip to extract the meat.

If you insist on deveining them first, twist the middle flap of the tail, them pull out straight. The intestine should slide right out.

"Sucking the heads" implies the removal of the "fat" (hepato-pancreas) by the eaters literally sucking it out. Spooning it out with a finger or knife works just as well and is recommended if you're collecting the fat to use in another recipe.

Crawfish are easier to peel when they're fresh and still warm. When you've eaten so much you can't get up from the table, go ahead and peel any leftovers for tomorrow's étouffée.

Finally, a word of warning: crawfish boiled in spicy water, and especially crawfish spiced after boiling, carry a lot of pepper that gets on your fingers, so *keep your fingers out of your eyes!* Forget vanity and take your contacts out *before* you start eating.

N U T R I T I O N A L   Q U A L I T I E S of crawfish represent a classic case of good news, bad news. Pound for pound, crawfish tail meat has about a third the calories of ground beef and is very low in fat, and some of that is omega 3, the "fish oil" that many believe promotes long life. Besides a lot of protein, crawfish also provide the minerals calcium, iron, and phosphorus and the vitamins thiamine, niacin, and riboflavin.

The bad news is the amount of cholesterol; the cooked mudbug has 178 milligrams per three and one-half-ounce serving. (The same serving has 1.35 grams fat and 114 calories.) But except in the few areas where crawfish are a seasonal staple, most people are not likely to eat them often. It's your daily behavior you have to watch. Most physicians will readily admit that when it comes to diet, what you do once in a while won't kill you.

A C C O M P A N I M E N T S to crawfish are often tossed in to cook with crawfish in the same pot. Just about everything but the kitchen toaster has been used, but the most common additions are shucked corn on the cob, potatoes, onions, garlic (peeled and whole), carrots, artichokes, whole hams, wieners or smoked sausage.

By now you're probably getting the idea. Anything you might normally boil, when its flavor isn't so subtle or consistency so fragile that it will be overwhelmed, is a good candidate for the crawfish pot. Bear in mind individual cooking times. Potatoes go in early, well before the crawfish. Fresh corn goes in late unless one likes it mushy.

While all of these foods will add flavor to the crawfish, mostly they pick up the spices in the water just as the crawfish do. Gulf blue crabs are sometimes boiled with crawfish, but be sure to put them in first because they take twice as long to cook.

Among Cajuns, side dishes are usually limited to an optional mayonnaise-ketchup or horseradish sauce and lots of French bread. Since this is a meal to be eaten with one's hands, it's best not to get too fancy.

B E V E R A G E S depend upon how the meal was cooked. A Cajun could no more enjoy a crawfish boil without beer than a Swede could without 80-proof aquavit. With more elaborate dishes, a chilled dry white wine is the standard seafood accompaniment. Chablis, sauvignon blanc, or a German reisling are often recommended.

Never serve an old-time Cajun milk with crawfish or other seafood, though, for the combination is considered quite unhealthful.

C L E A N - U P is easy if you covered your table with newspapers. Roll them up with the empty crawfish shells inside. If you ate outside, hose everything down. Don't miss the garbage man! Few things smell as bad as decaying crawfish hulls.

Some folks use crawfish as garden compost, which is admirable, but bear in mind their (temporary but potent) smell and the fact that until they are well-leached by rainfall, the salt they picked up from the cooking water can damage tender plants.

CLEANING YOUR HANDS is important, or else the next day folks will know you had a crawfish boil and will be upset that you didn't invite them. After a good soap-and-water treatment, wash your hands again in lemon juice, if needed. Some old timers recommend a scouring with salt.

FREEZING is the way to go if you want to keep crawfish more than twenty-four hours. Keeping them as long as three to four days in the refrigerator is usually safe, but why take chances?

Freezing crawfish whole works fine, especially if they are in water, but they do take up more room that way, so most people peel them, or at least break off the heads first. As opposed to whole crawfish, peeled tails are best frozen dry. (Water makes them mushy.) A dip in a very mild solution of lemon juice prevents the harmless color change (they turn blue) that will sometimes occur.

Crawfish "fat" adds flavor to many recipes, but if you'll be keeping them frozen for more than a couple of weeks, you'd do best to wash off all the fat before freezing, since even frozen crawfish fat can quickly become rancid. Washed crawfish tails can last a year in the freezer without losing flavor.

OTHER CRAWFISH DISHES are limited only by your imagination. An international sampling follows, but don't let that limit you. A 1992 newspaper survey of the finer New Orleans restaurants found them serving crawfish fettucine, crawfish en croute, and crawfish mousse, among many other selections.

If you like using ethnic cookbooks, remember that for any

European country with limited access to the ocean—Austria, Czechoslovakia, Hungary, Russia, Switzerland—recipes calling for shrimp or crab were probably originally cooked with crawfish, and the substitution can easily be made.

Note that cooking crawfish meat in a cast-iron pot will sometimes discolor it, which may be less pleasing to the eye but is in no way harmful.

S O F T - S H E L L   C R A W F I S H are still not as easy to find as live or peeled crawfish, but their texture and flavor, reminiscent of soft-shell crabs, make them worth tracking down.

To prepare them for cooking, cut across the shell just behind the eyes and discard the top part of the head. Squeeze the body gently and the two "lucky stones" (calcium deposits) will slide out, leaving the "softie" ready for battering, marinating, stuffing or whatever else might be called for in your favorite recipe.

E A T I N G   O U T may be the only recourse for those who've become exhausted merely reading the instructions above. When this chapter began, you got a line and I got a pole, Baby. Now we're waiting for menus. As the popularity of crawfish increases, chefs continue to find new and intriguing ways to cook and serve them. Choosing is purely a matter of individual taste.

If you're fortunate enough to find yourself traveling on Interstate 10 an hour west of Baton Rouge or half that distance east of Lafayette, do stop in at Henderson, which, whatever other towns might claim, is certainly the crawfish *restaurant* capital of the world. Any of the Henderson eateries can serve you a good meal, but pros recommend Pat's for tradition, Robin's for étouffée or gumbo, and McGee's Landing for its beautiful view—across the levee, it literally hangs over the lapping waters of the Atchafalaya Basin and is very romantic. If you are shopping for the best deal on a platter of boiled crawfish, follow the signs. Price wars are frequent and frequently intense.

Though it's usually the most expensive thing on the menu, the crawfish platter is the best bet for novices who don't yet know their favorites. If your wallet or belt won't stretch that far, buy one and split it between two people.

Then, eat and enjoy!

RECIPES

CRAWFISH BOILING RECIPES

Baboo Guidry's Boiled Crawfish to Serve 20,000

Makes 20,000 servings.

That's right, 20,000 people! Figuring 3 pounds per person, that's 30 tons of crawfish. Baboo Guidry once cooked that much at a shindig for a Houston manufacturer of blow-out preventors.* Most people never throw a party that size, but Baboo's tricks can be adapted to any large gathering. After all, you cook them in "small" batches. For the first batch you'll need:

> *700 pounds live crawfish*
> *15 pounds cayenne pepper*
> *60 pounds salt*
> *½ gallon liquid crab boil seasoning*

Obviously, you'll also need some serious equipment: a high-pressure gas burner, a double-walled kettle that traps the heat in its sides, a stirring paddle, a heavy-duty boiling basket and a hoist to lift it.

---

*"Blow-out preventors" are not party-poopers (as such a gathering proves) but rather oilfield safety devices.

Put in crawfish and let boil for ten minutes after water resumes boiling.

For batches 2–4, use half as much pepper, salt and seasoning. By this point your water is getting pretty murky, and sideline coaches are suggesting you dump it and heat up a new batch. Don't. It's not necessary and would take so long your hungry guests would riot. For batch 5, you don't need any spices, nor crawfish either, because this one consists of (and here's the secret):

500 pounds whole corn on the cob.

Not only does the spiced, boiled corn go well with crawfish, but more importantly it filters your water, clearing the grit and cloudiness. After that, respice your water as if you were at the first batch, and start the cycle over.

Cajun Crawfish Boil

Okay, so you don't have 20,000 close friends. If you're slightly less ambitious, and are willing to settle for a sack, here goes:

25 to 30 pounds live crawfish
1½ to 2 boxes salt
6 bags crab/crawfish boil
1 small bottle liquid crab boil
6 ears of corn, cut in half
8 to 10 red potatoes
2 whole pods of garlic
2 lemons cut in half

4 whole onions
¼ to ½ cup red pepper

Put crawfish in a tub or plastic kiddy pool filled with water. Let them soak clean (in the shade if possible) for as long as it takes to get everything else ready. Make sure your boiling pot is large enough to hold crawfish and water to cover them by at least 2 inches.

Fill the pot with clean water. Add everything except crawfish and bring the water to a boil. Drain crawfish, then add them to the boiling pot, stirring them around. Let the water come back to full boil, cover, then *check your watch*. Crawfish should boil 5 to 7 minutes (depending on size) and *no longer* for easy peeling.

Turn the fire off and let stand with lid on for 15 to 20 minutes. Do a taste test. If needed, add more salt and red pepper, then soak a few more minutes. Drain crawfish and dump them onto a newspaper-covered table. Add a couple of bowls of sauce (see recipes) and grab a chilled brew. Chow time!

Note: Average 3 to 5 pounds crawfish per person.

SIDE SAUCES FOR CAJUN CRAWFISH BOILS

New Orleans Crawfish Sauce

This standard concoction can be found from Houston to New Orleans and is equally great with raw oysters or boiled shrimp.

> *2 cups ketchup*
> *2 tablespoons horseradish*
> *2 tablespoons Worcestershire*
> *2 tablespoons water*
> *Tabasco to taste*

Combine all ingredients. Refrigerate until needed.

Down Bayou Lafourche Crawfish Sauce

In Gulf Coast fishing communities, where crawfish help mark time until the blessing of the fleet inaugurates shrimp season, this milder sauce is used on both.

> *1 cup mayonnaise*
> *1 cup ketchup*

¼ cup finely chopped onion
¼ cup dill relish
Salt and pepper to taste

Mix all ingredients. Refrigerate.

Oregon-Style Crawfish Boiled in Pickling Spices

Makes 1 meal-by-itself serving.

Delores Abernathy described the way the old timers taught the youngsters to cook crawfish when the Tualatin Crawfish Festival began in 1951:

5 pounds crawfish
1 cup salt
½ cup pickling spices in an herb bag
½ cup vinegar

Bring to a boil enough seasoned water to cover crawfish. Add crawfish. Return to a boil for 10 minutes. Remove crawfish and immerse in cold water to halt cooking. When the spiced cooking water cools down, return the crawfish to it. Refrigerate and let them marinate for 1 hour up to 1 day. Drain and let them warm to room temperature before serving.

Kicki's Scandinavian-Style Crawfish Boiled with Dill

Makes 12 servings.

Kicki Mazur (yes, the same Kicki we met in Chapter 7), Gudrun Merrill and Birgitta Paino are three pillars of the Swedish community in Houston. They were gracious enough to invite me over to watch how they make this recipe, which Kicki learned from her grandmother.

The women noted that crawfish season in Sweden (beginning August 8) marks the last of the bearably warm weather. In Texas, a spring crawfish season signals the last of the bearably cool weather.

> *10 pounds live crawfish*
> *¾ cup salt*
> *6 cups fresh dill*
> *8 ounces beer*
> *1 lump sugar*

Wash and purge the crawfish. If they're particularly muddy, do it twice. (Swedes catch crawfish in rock streams and find a muddy taste objectionable.)

Add the salt, beer, sugar, and 4 cups of dill to 3 gallons of water and bring it a quick boil. Flowering dill is best. Toss in stems, flowers and all. Dill seed can supplement but not replace fresh if all the fresh you can find seems wimpy.

When the cauldron is bubbling, add the crawfish and cover. Let the water come back to a fast boil, count off 2 minutes, then turn off the burner. Let the crawfish cool *in the same water.* When they're cool enough, put the whole pot into the refrigerator at least overnight and up to 48 hours, leaving them to marinate the whole time in the water in which they boiled.

It should be noted that many Scandinavian cooks save the actual crowns for decoration and after boiling strain out the cooked dill so it can be replaced with fresh before chilling.

Drain the crawfish, let them warm to room temperature, then

arrange them decoratively on a tray using the remaining dill crowns as garnish.

Each tail should be eaten on buttered toast (toasted French bread is about right) and served with caraway seed cheese (*"kryddost"*). Wash it down with beer, white wine or iced schnapps. Each place setting should have a finger bowl with a lemon wedge, bib and napkin. Cantaloupe and raspberries are a traditional dessert. *Skål!*

CRAWFISH SALADS

If you ate too much at your crawfish boil *and* you still have some left over, salads are the perfect solution. Here are a couple of favorites, but use your imagination.

Italian Style Crawfish Salad

Makes 2 meal salads or 4 side salads.

To this mixture can be added pasta or rice for a delicious cold salad.

½ pound crawfish tails
½ cup celery, chopped
½ cup bell pepper, chopped
½ cup green onions, chopped
¼ cup parsley
¼ cup green or black olives, chopped
½ cup Italian-style dressing

Mix all ingredients, chill overnight. Toss with 2 cups cooked rice or 4 cups cooked rotini pasta. Serve over lettuce with sliced tomato or avocado.

Crawfish Waldorf Salad

Makes 4 generous servings.

Here's a crawfish salad that's easy and refreshing, yet classy.

1 pound crawfish tails
2 medium apples, diced
½ cup walnuts, chopped
1 cup mayonnaise
¼ teaspoon tarragon
Salt, pepper, lemon juice, and paprika to taste

Combine all ingredients. Serve over shredded lettuce.

LOUISIANA CRAWFISH RECIPES

The Original Etouffée

Makes 2 servings.

This dish is so common and beloved nowadays that most people believe crawfish étouffée has been around forever. Not so! Crawfish gumbo may go back 200 years and crawfish bisque farther than that, but crawfish étouffée is a product of the middle 20th Century.

Around Breaux Bridge, Catahoula and Henderson (where they really ought to know) most people credit Mrs. Aline Champagne with inventing the dish. Madame Aline says that the recipe below is about the way she first cooked it in the 1950s at the Rendez-Vous Restaurant in Breaux Bridge.

> *1 cup chopped onion*
> *2 tablespoons oil*
> *1 cup crawfish tail meat with fat*
> *¾ cup water*
> *1 rounded tablespoon flour*
> *Paprika, salt, red and black pepper to taste*
> *Parsley and green onion, chopped for garnish*

Sauté onion in oil until golden and tender. Add water and tails with fat. Simmer for 15 to 20 minutes. Thicken with flour, add seasonings to taste. Serve over rice. Garnish with parsley and green onion. Quick and easy.

Edwin Edward's Brown Etouffée

Makes 6 servings.

Everybody's étouffée is different. Louisiana's four-term Cajun governor offers here his favorite étouffée recipe, which is based on a dark roux.

½ cup butter or margarine
⅓ cup all-purpose flour
1 cup each onions, celery and green peppers, chopped
2 cloves garlic, minced
3 cups crawfish tails (12 ounces)
2 cups chicken broth
¼ cup chopped parsley
1 teaspoon salt
⅛ teaspoon ground black pepper
⅛ teaspoon red pepper

Melt butter in large heavy pot. Blend flour and stir over medium-low heat, until roux is dark brown (10 to 15 minutes).

Add onions, celery, green peppers, and garlic. Cook until tender-crisp, 2 to 3 minutes.

Stir in remaining ingredients and simmer 20 minutes. Ladle into soup bowls and top each serving with ½ cup rice.

Yvonne's Deluxe Red Etouffée

Makes 8 servings.

There are as many recipes for crawfish étouffée in Louisiana as there are cooks. This is beginning to be true out of state as well. Yvonne Hall is one of those dedicated individuals who is making Texas safe for Cajun culture. Her sumptuous red étouffée is sure to increase your assortment of spices.

1½ pound crawfish tails
2 stalks green onion, chopped
1 medium white onion, chopped
2 stalks celery, chopped
½ medium green bell pepper, chopped
2 cloves garlic, crushed
¼ cup parsley
1 small tomato, chopped (use only if red and ripe)
3 cups vegetable broth (2 vegetable bouillon cubes to
*   3 cups boiling water)*

SEASONINGS:
¾ teaspoon salt
⅛ teaspoon Beau Monde
¼ teaspoon Old Bay
¼ teaspoon curry powder
½ teaspoon cayenne pepper
½ teaspoon seasoned salt
½ teaspoon paprika
½ teaspoon thyme
2 to 4 drops Tabasco sauce

ROUX:
½ cup real butter (lightly salted variety)
⅓ cup flour

GARNISH:
¼ cup parsley
1 stalk green onion, chopped

Combine roux ingredients and brown to a delicate, light caramel color—not a dark gumbo roux. Add freshly chopped vegetables (stand back as this makes quite a sizzle), and continue stirring. Add hot broth. Reduce heat and add seasonings. Let simmer 15 to 20 minutes. Add crawfish and let cook another 15 to 20 minutes for a sumptuous red étouffée! Serve over Louisiana rice and sprinkle with garnish.

Suggestions: Serve French bread and a crisp salad on the side. Use hot broth or roux will separate. Do not use a cast-iron pot unless you want a brown étouffée.

Lafcadio Hearn's Crawfish Bisque

Makes 4 servings.

Man-of-letters and gastronome extraordinaire Lafcadio Hearn was a $10-a-week writer for the New Orleans Item when he compiled *La Cuisine Créole*. First published in 1880, it predated the Cajun food fad by a century. This prototypical cookbook (reprinted by Pelican as the *Creole Cook Book*) belongs in every serious cook's collection.

The recipe that follows is Hearn's version of Crayfish Bisque—a Creole Dish, adapted here for the modern kitchen.

STUFFING:

3 pounds crawfish, enough to yield ½ pound meat
3 to 4 ounces French bread soaked in milk
¼ pound butter, melted
1 clove garlic, minced
Salt, thyme, sage to taste
1 small onion, chopped
flour

Rinse crawfish well, then parboil. Separate tail meat, put aside.
Clean the crawfish carapace (the curled, rounded piece of the shell
that covers the upper back—looks kind of like a small red taco),
discarding head and claws; soak in salt water for 2 to 3 minutes,
then drain. After mincing tail meat, combine with additional ingredients and cook 10 minutes, stirring continually. Stuff drained
shells with mixture, roll in flour and fry lightly.

STOCK:

3 tablespoons butter
Slice of bacon, chopped
2 small onions, chopped
Flour
1½ pint boiling water or beef stock
Salt, pepper, thyme to taste
1 bay leaf

Sauté onions with bacon and butter. Sprinkle with enough flour to
absorb grease. Cook to golden color. Add water or stock, along with
seasonings. Simmer 30 minutes. Add stuffed heads, then cook
another 15 minutes. Serve with rice.

Sydney Guidry's Crawfish Gumbo

Makes 6 servings.

This delightful dish was inspired by Sydney Guidry of Catahoula, Louisiana, who said that after the flood of 1927, since there were so many crawfish and they were biting everyone's toes, they *had* to be eaten.

½ cup oil
½ cup flour
1 large onion, chopped
½ cup celery, chopped
3 garlic cloves, minced
¼ cup crawfish fat (optional)
¼ cup green onions, chopped
¼ cup parsley, chopped
1 pound crawfish tail meat with fat
4 to 6 cups hot chicken broth or water

In a cast-iron dutch oven, combine oil and flour. Cook to make a dark brown roux. Add onion, celery, and garlic, and cook until tender. Stir in hot water or broth to desired thickness. Add seasonings. Simmer 30 minutes. Add tails, green onion and parsley, and simmer 20 minutes. Serve over rice with filé (dried ground sassafras leaves) and hot sauce within reach.

Tante Mimi's Easy-as-Crawfish Pie

Makes 6 servings.

Tante Mimi played Hank Williams's song about "jambalaya, crawfish pie, filé gumbo" over and over and over again until finally Nonc' Hol put the record under a sofa cushion and said, " Honey, why don't you come sit down by me?"

Traditional pie recipes call for lots of butter and cream. This is a "light" alternative, part of the "diet" Tante Mimi fashioned for Nonc' Hol after she found her record broken.

> *1 pound crawfish tail meat*
> *¾ stick of margarine*
> *1 cup chopped onion*
> *½ cup chopped green onion*
> *½ cup chopped bell pepper*
> *½ cup chopped celery*
> *¼ cup chopped parsley*
> *2 cloves garlic, minced*
> *3 tablespoons flour*
> *1 cup evaporated skimmed milk*
> *Salt, black pepper and red pepper to taste*
> *9-inch pie shell (bake for 5 minutes before filling)*

Sauté onion, green onion, celery, bell pepper, parsley, and garlic in margarine until clear. Add evaporated skimmed milk and flour. Stir continually and simmer until well blended. Add tails. Pour mixture in pie shell. Bake at 350° for 30 minutes. Let stand 5 minutes before serving.

Big Randy's Battered Tails

Makes 4 servings.

Golden Meadow, Louisiana, is home port to scores of shrimp boats. Randolph's Cafe has long been lauded as the town's best restaurant. So it was a surprise to many when, as Randolph, Sr. began surrendering the kitchen to Randolph, Jr., crawfish made it to the menu alongside all the traditional fresh Gulf seafood. Taste this dish, and you'll agree that it's not just a surprise, but a delight.

> *1 tablespoon Zatarain's Creole Seasoning*
> *1 cup buttermilk*
> *Dash of hot sauce*
> *1 pound crawfish tails with fat*
> *2 cups fine corn flour*
> *Cooking oil to cover*

Blend first 3 ingredients. Soak tails in mixture, then roll in corn flour. Deep-fry in batches at 350° for just 1 or 2 minutes. Serve hot. Delicious!

This recipe works equally well with soft-shell crawfish. Marinate them first for three hours in buttermilk.

Crawfish Croustade

Serves 6.

What happens when you turn the master chef of a fine Creole restaurant loose on a Cajun staple like crawfish pie? If you're lucky, you get a dish like this one. From that uptown New Orleans landmark restaurant, Commander's Palace, comes this treasure that proves haute cuisine need not be complicated to prepare.

> *2 pounds crawfish, shelled (tail meat only)*
> *2 teaspoons Creole seafood seasoning*
> *6 ounces butter*
> *¼ cup minced shallots*
> *½ cup dry white wine*
> *3 cups shrimp or fish stock*
> *1 cup whipping cream*
> *6 puff pastry shells (can be obtained from bakery)*

Season crawfish with Creole seafood seasoning. Heat half the butter in a heavy iron skillet. Add shallots and sauté until shallots are transparent. Add crawfish and cook for two minutes. Remove crawfish and keep warm.

Add the wine to juices and shallots remaining in pan and cook, stirring, for 1 minute. Add the stock and cook until reduced by half. Add cream and continue to cook until sauce is reduced by half. Add remaining butter and swirl pan above the heat until butter is melted and sauce is glazed. Add crawfish to sauce and simmer for 2 minutes longer. Serve in pastry shells.

Hal Beridon's Eggplant St. Julien

Makes 6 servings.

This recipe was devised by Troy Meacham, executive chef at the Lafayette Hilton and Towers in Lafayette, Louisiana, but it was my old friend Hal Beridon, the hotel manager, who twisted Troy's arm until he revealed his secrets.

This is one of those recipes that starts with traditional Cajun ingredients such as crawfish and eggplant but then takes them to such heights of culinary artistry that you'd never guess their ancestry was simple country cooking.

STUFFING:
¼ pound margarine
½ pound chopped onions
¼ pound chopped bell peppers
2 tablespoons chopped garlic
1 pound peeled crawfish tails
1 teaspoon dried basil
1 teaspoon dried thyme
⅛ teaspoon cayenne pepper
¼ cup bread crumbs
¼ cup parmesan cheese

EGGPLANT CUTLETS:
3 eggplants
3 cups flour
2 cups milk
4 whole eggs
3 cups Italian bread crumbs
¼ pound margarine

HOLLANDAISE SAUCE:
1 pound unsalted butter
6 egg yolks

2 tablespoons lemon juice
Pinch of cayenne
Salt to taste

Stuffing: Heat margarine in a large skillet until it begins to turn brown. Add onions and sauté until they are translucent. Then add bell peppers, celery and garlic, and sauté until celery becomes tender.

Add the crawfish tails, basil, thyme and cayenne pepper. Continue to sauté, combining all the ingredients thoroughly. When everything is hot, pour the mixture into a colander to remove the excess liquid and grease, then pour it into a bowl. Add the parmesan cheese and bread crumbs. Mix thoroughly and set aside.

Eggplant cutlets: Wash the eggplants, then cut them into ½" slices, at least 4 per eggplant. (Peeling is optional.) Dredge each cutlet in flour. Handling them as little as possible, use a fork to force the cutlets into a wash made from whole eggs and milk. When they are completely covered with milk, dredge them in the bread crumbs until completely coated.

Heat margarine in a skillet to frying temperature. Panfry the cutlets until light brown on both sides, then place them on a paper towel to absorb excess grease.

Place 6 cutlets on a cookie sheet. Put a 4-ounce scoop of the stuffing in the center of each. Cover the scoops with the remaining cutlets, forming sandwiches. Bake the eggplant-and-stuffing sandwiches in a 300° oven for 20 minutes.

Sauce: Melt the butter in a saucepan and bring it to a simmer. While butter is melting, whip 6 egg yolks in a mixing bowl with an electric mixer. When butter has reached a constant simmer begin very slowly drizzling it over the egg yolks as you continue to whip them. When all the butter has mixed into the egg, add the lemon juice, cayenne pepper, and salt.

Serving: Remove the eggplant sandwiches from the oven and arrange them on the serving plates. Top each with hollandaise sauce and serve immediately.

Sauté of Louisiana Crawfish

Serves 4.

A crawfish feast need not be a major undertaking. Here is a simple, very tasty, and exceptionally versatile way to prepare crawfish. The resulting sauce goes equally well over pasta, rice, or whatever you like. Use your imagination. And lest you worry that it's *too* easy, bear in mind that this same dish is served at Commander's Palace, the restaurant that many connoisseurs believe is the finest in New Orleans.

> *1 pound cooked crawfish tails, peeled and deveined*
> *1 cup green onions, chopped*
> *1 tablespoon Creole seafood seasoning*
> *1 tablespoon Worcestershire sauce*
> *9 ounces soft butter (2 sticks plus 2 tablespoons)*

In a frying pan, sauté crawfish tails and green onions in the 2 tablespoons of butter with seafood seasoning and Worcestershire sauce until hot, stirring constantly. Remove from heat. Add the remaining butter, tossing mixture gently until the butter is incorporated and the sauce is creamy. Serve over crawfish cakes, rice or pasta.

Broiled Soft-Shell Crawfish

Serves 4 to 6.

2 dozen soft-shell crawfish
2 cups dry sherry
1 teaspoon creole seasoning
½ cup prepared mustard
4 tablespoons butter
Dash lemon juice

Mix the sherry, mustard, and creole seasoning into a marinade. Cover the cleaned softies and marinate in the refrigerator for at least four hours.

To cook, take the crawfish out of the marinade and place on a broiler pan. Drizzle half the butter and lemon juice, and then broil for 3 or 4 minutes. Turn over and repeat.

RECIPES FROM AROUND THE WORLD

Crawfish Nantua

Makes 4 very filling servings, or 8 to 12 appetizer portions.

This is a classic, very rich (and very complicated) French dish. If you were inspired by the story of how the French of *la Belle Epoque* employed crawfish to assure seduction, remember that a century has passed since then. Boiled mudbugs will no longer cut it. But a dish like this just might!

> *1 pound crawfish meat*
> *3 tablespoons butter*
> *1 tablespoon chopped shallots*
> *¼ teaspoon salt*
> *Dash of cayenne*
> *3 tablespoons cognac*
>
> NANTUA SAUCE:
> *4 tablespoons butter*
> *6 tablespoon flour*
> *1 teaspoon salt*

¼ teaspoon white pepper
2 cups hot milk
½ cup cream
1 small onion, finely chopped
¼ cup crawfish butter (see recipe to follow)

HOLLANDAISE SAUCE:
4 egg yolks
2 tablespoons cream
1 tablespoon fresh lemon juice
⅛ teaspoon salt
Dash of cayenne
½ pound soft butter

Nantua sauce: Melt butter in skillet. Add flour, salt and white pepper. Blend thoroughly. Remove skillet from heat and add 2 cups hot milk. Stirring continually, return to heat for a few minutes until thickened. Add cream and finely chopped onion. Cook over very low flame for an hour, stirring occasionally. Add crawfish butter and set aside.

Hollandaise sauce: Combine egg yolks, cream, lemon juice, salt and a dash of cayenne. In a double boiler, stir until thickened. Whip in ½ pound soft butter. Set aside.

Sauté crawfish meat in butter with chopped shallots, salt and a dash of cayenne. Add cognac and ignite. Stir until extinguished. Blend in Nantua sauce. Remove from heat and add hollandaise. Pour into individual serving dishes (or one shallow dish) and place under broiler until golden brown.

Ecrevisses à La Montagneuse

Makes 2 servings.

While working on this book, I drove my wife, family and friends crazy by talking about nothing but crawfish. After they began to shun me, I found myself one day at the Café du Monde in the New Orleans French Quarter striking up a crawfish conversation with a group of strangers. I was delighted to find that they were French tourists who could offer me this sample of easy home cooking from southern France.

> *½ pound crawfish tail meat*
> *1 small onion, chopped*
> *4 tablespoons cognac*
> *¼ cup butter*
> *¼ cup olive oil*
> *2 cloves garlic, minced*
> *1 small can tomato sauce*
> *¼ cup white wine*
> *Salt and black pepper to taste*

Sauté crawfish in olive oil and butter. Add chopped onion and sauté 5 more minutes. Remove from fire, add cognac, then ignite. Stir until extinguished. Add tomato sauce, wine, and other seasonings to taste. Serve with rice.

Crawfish Court Bouillon

Makes 6 servings.

Court bouillon means "short boil," and that's essentially the idea behind this French dish, also known as Ecrevisses à la Nage. It's one of those fun dishes that you eat with a spoon until there's no more liquid; then you pick up the crawfish and continue with your fingers.

> *2 dozen clean crawfish*
> *2 cups white wine*
> *2 cups water*
> *1 large onion, chopped*
> *2 large carrots, sliced*
> *¼ teaspoon thyme*
> *¼ teaspoon dill*
> *1 bay leaf*
> *3 or 4 cloves*
> *Salt, black pepper and red pepper to taste*

Bring all ingredients, except crawfish, to a boil in a large pot, then simmer until carrots are almost tender. Return to a boil and add crawfish. Boil covered another 7 minutes. Serve in bowls garnished with parsley sprigs.

Crawfish Vienna (cooked in beer)

Makes 4 servings.

Austrians like beer as much as their German cousins to the north do. Follow this recipe and you will, too.

3 pounds large crawfish (about 3 dozen)
2 quarts beer
1 tablespoon caraway seeds
½ cup parsley
Salt to taste

Chill crawfish to anesthetize them. Devein them by twisting the middle tail flap, then pulling out straight. If this procedure seems too cruel (or too complicated), you can instead purge the crawfish by immersing them at least 10 minutes in very salty water. In either case, follow up with a good cleaning by brushing them well under running water.

For 10 minutes boil the crawfish in enough light beer to cover, along with parsley, caraway seeds and salt. Lift crawfish into a large tureen, then strain the beer stock over them. Enjoy!

Crawfish Butter

This is an East European version of a condiment loved in France as well. It's a good way to use the rest of the crawfish after you've taken the meat from them for use in another recipe. The quantities of ingredients depend on how many crawfish you have.

Crawfish shells with fat
Melted butter
Paprika to taste

Cut off and discard the front of the crawfish head, including the eyes, horns, and the two disc-shaped "lucky stones" inside. Take the remaining shells and fat and crush them thoroughly with a mortar and pestle or blender. In a food processor, blend shells with an equal portion of warm butter. Add paprika. Strain mixture and chill. It'll be pink and rich and tasty.

For a more French-style crawfish butter, leave out the paprika.

Budapest Crawfish Soup

Makes 4 servings.

Elek Magyar was a famous Hungarian journalist, primarily a food writer, who lived in Budapest between World Wars I and II. The recipe that follows is based on one of his favorite dishes. Magyar wrote that the crawfish soup served at a restaurant on Budapest City Park "was a more reliable attraction than primadonnas at the City Park Theatre."

STOCK:
¼ cup parsley
1 tablespoon caraway seeds
1 tablespoon peppercorns
1 teaspoon salt
4 pounds crawfish
3 egg yolks
⅓ cup flour
⅓ cup butter
2 tablespoons brandy
¼ cup white wine
½ teaspoon salt

Boil crawfish for 10 minutes in salted water with an herb bag of parsley, caraway seeds and peppercorns. Remove crawfish, reserve stock. Peel crawfish. Stir egg yolks in with the meat, add a sprinkle of flour and 1 tablespoon melted butter. Set aside.

Use remaining shell for crawfish butter (see previous recipe), reserving if you wish a dozen carapaces to stuff for soup garnish.

Make a light roux with flour and butter. Add paprika, ¼ cup crawfish butter, brandy, white wine, and salt. Stir in crawfish meat mixture over low flame. Add crawfish stock to thin. Serve in bowls.

If you wish to garnish with stuffed shells, any number of stuffings would go well with this dish. A nice combination of rice, mincemeat and cheese (flavored with paprika, of course) would delight even a Hungarian traditionalist.

Hungarian Paprika Crawfish

Makes 2 servings.

In New Orleans oysters are eaten only in months with an *r* in their name. In Hungary, the opposite applies to crawfish, whose season there begins in May and runs through August. Here is a recipe your author and his wife picked up while honeymooning near Lake Balaton in central Hungary. It's easier than the preceding soup.

4 pounds crawfish
½ cup grated onion
¼ cup butter
2 teaspoons paprika
A pinch of salt

HERB BAG:

2 tablespoons caraway seeds

2 tablespoons peppercorns

Boil crawfish in salted water with an herb bag of caraway seeds and peppercorns. Lift out crawfish and peel meat, add to ½ cup grated onion and ¼ cup butter. Sauté for 10 minutes. Thin with crawfish stock. Add paprika and salt to taste.

Crawfish Russe

Makes 2 servings.

Russians have always been crawfish-loving people. Crawfish frequent their folklore, and their cuisine. This dish is a lot like the French court bouillon but is simpler, with a more crawfish-y flavor.

1 dozen crawfish

1 carrot, sliced

1 onion, chopped

4 cups water or broth

Sprig of parsley

Sprig of dill

1 bay leaf

Salt and pepper to taste

Put clean crawfish in saucepan. Cover with 4 cups water or broth. Add carrots, onion, parsley, dill and bay leaf. Cook for 15 to 20 minutes. Season to taste. Spoon into bowls.

Australian Crawfish in Banana Leaves

Makes 4 servings.

This dish is based on an Australian recipe that calls for 3 crawfish to serve 6 people! Yes, the crawfish really do get that big down there. Here's a version that's altered to accommodate our smaller U.S. varieties.

> *3 dozen crawfish*
> *4 large banana leaves*
> *½ pound softened butter*
> *2 cups champagne or white wine*

Parboil crawfish in lightly salted water for no more than a few minutes—this is not to cook them but to render them unable to crawl out of the banana leaves.

Lay banana leaves in a shallow baking dish, spread with butter. Place crawfish on center of each leaf, pour champagne or wine over them. Fold leaf around each batch and tie with string. Bake at 325° for ½ hour.

Szechuan Ginger Crawfish

Makes 4 servings.

The idea for this recipe came from a shrimp dish in a Chinese-American cookbook. Giving some background, the book's author said that she based her recipe on one that originated in Szechuan, China, where, far from the ocean, shrimp were unknown. Local cooks who wanted shellfish caught crawfish instead.

This version of the recipe goes back to the original.

> *1 pound crawfish tails, deveined and defatted*
> *¼ cup fresh ginger, minced*
> *½ bunch green onions, chopped*
> *1 teaspoon salt*
> *1/4 teaspoon sugar*
> *2 tablespoons oil*
> *3 tablespoons cooking sherry*

Combine all ingredients except oil in a bowl. Mix well and let marinate for at least 30 minutes. Heat oil until very hot, add mixture and stir-fry for 3 to 4 minutes. Add sherry and cover the pot (or better yet, the wok), reduce heat and let simmer 2 minutes. Serve with white rice.

Crawfish Tempura

Makes 2 servings.

The name implies a Japanese ancestry for this dish, but actually we jazzed this one up after reading Euell Gibbons's *Stalking the Wild Asparagus.* Kind of tastes like a wild hickory nut (just kidding).

Though Gibbons was following a long-standing midwestern tradition, the result is a lot like the way you'd see shrimp (and other foods such as vegetables) cooked in a fine Japanese restaurant.

This recipe would work equally well with soft-shell crawfish. If they are large, cut them into chunks.

> *½ pound crawfish tailmeat*
> *2 eggs, beaten*
> *¼ cup water*

1 cup biscuit mix
½ teaspoon salt
⅛ teaspoon red pepper
⅛ teaspoon black pepper
Cooking oil to cover

Make a batter with the ingredients, then dip the tails. Fry in enough oil to cover at medium-high heat for 2 to 3 minutes. Drain and serve.

As long as you're at it, why not take a hint from the Japanese and extend this dish by frying up some carrots, broccoli, and bell pepper in the same batter and oil?

Glen's Crawfish Maki

Makes about 20 pieces.

Frankly this is one of my favorite things to do with leftovers from a crawfish boil. It's also the only dish I know that uses peeled tails where you still get to eat with your hands. (Even the Japanese don't use chopsticks for sushi rolls!)

You may have to seek out an oriental grocery or gourmet shop to find the nori (paper-thin sheets of seaweed), wasabi (often called Japanese horseradish) and pickled ginger.

1 cup short grain rice, uncooked
1½ cup water
2 tablespoons rice vinegar (tarragon or cider is acceptable substitute)
2 tablespoons sugar

1 teaspoon salt
¾ cup deveined, defatted cooked crawfish tails, chopped
    coarsely
4 strips green onion
½ peeled cucumber, cut in long, narrow strips
Parsley, chopped fine
Nori (seaweed roll)

CONDIMENTS:
Wasabi
Pickled ginger, thinly sliced
Light soy sauce

If using powdered wasabi (horseradish), mix a tablespoon full with enough water to make a paste. Let stand while preparing sushi.

Rinse the rice until water becomes clear. Add drained rice to water and boil for 3 minutes. Then cover and simmer for 15 minutes or until there's no more water. While cooking rice, put vinegar, salt and sugar into a small pan; heat until combined, then let cool.

Pour cooked rice onto a flat tray and spread it thinly and evenly with a spatula. Run spatula back and forth through grains to separate them while pouring vinegar mix over rice. Avoid adding too much, or the rice may become mushy. Let stand at room temperature until ready to use.

Take a sheet of nori and a flat surface (or bamboo mat if you have one). Spread rice lengthwise in middle of nori. Make a slight well in center of rice and put down a strip of green onion and one of cucumber. Lay crawfish on top (note: never use raw crawfish) and sprinkle lightly with finely chopped parsley. Roll nori. Use a dab of water to "glue" nori if needed.

Using a very sharp knife, cut into 1½-inch lengths. Serve with small dishes of soy sauce, a little mound of wasabi and some pickled ginger.

Fettucini Ignace

Makes 4 servings.

There are many fancy new, non-traditional crawfish recipes. Here's one with an Italian flavor. It's fairly easy to make and tastes great. Since its creator wishes to remain anonymous, I've named it Fettucini Ignace, after a pet billy goat.

> *1 cup carrots, cut on the diagonal*
> *2 cups broccoli flowerets*
> *1 stick margarine*
> *2 cups crawfish tails, cleaned and deveined*
> *2 cloves garlic, pressed*
> *¼ teaspoon curry powder*
> *1 cup half-and-half*
> *2 tablespoons flour*
> *1 4-ounce jar diced pimientos, drained*
> *8 ounces fettucini, uncooked*
> *Salt and pepper to taste*

Start a large pot of salted water to boil for fettucini, and begin to steam carrots and broccoli in another. In a skillet melt margarine, add garlic, curry and tails, then sauté several minutes.

Water should be boiling by now so put fettucini in to cook, adding a dollop of olive oil to prevent sticking. If vegetables are tender, turn flame off and set aside. Add the half-and-half to the tails, and increase the heat to get a low boil, stirring continually. Add flour to thicken, salt and pepper to taste.

Remove from flame and add pimientos. Drain fettucini and put in large serving dish. Pour sauce over fettucini, add carrots and broccoli, then toss.

Just add a side salad and you have a complete gourmet meal.

Crawfish Sausage

Makes 4 rich servings.

A few years back, while I was director of the Louisiana Film Commission, I became well acquainted with the Windsor Court Hotel in New Orleans because many movie producers and stars insisted on staying there. In a city of many fine hotels, the Windsor Court is arguably the ritziest. Recipes like the one below help explain why.

Here's a dish that's as tasty as it is unconventional, from the Windsor Court's award-winning, internationally recognized chef, Kevin Graham.

> *1 pound cooked crawfish tails*
> *½ pound raw redfish fillet*
> *3 large egg whites*
> *Salt to taste*
> *Black pepper to taste*
> *2 cups heavy cream*

2 tablespoons brandy
½ teaspoon cayenne pepper, or to taste
¼ cup finely chopped scallions, green part only
½ onion, sliced
1 bay leaf
1 teaspoon black peppercorns
Cayenne Buerre Blanc (recipe follows)

Puree ½ pound of crawfish tails with the redfish in a food processor. With the machine running, add the egg whites. When the egg whites are thoroughly incorporated, add a generous pinch of salt to firm the mixture. (Salt coagulates protein. After salt is added, there will be a definite change in texture.) Season with black pepper to taste. With machine still running, gradually add the cream.

Transfer the mixture to a bowl and fold in brandy, cayenne pepper, the scallions and the remaining ½ pound of crawfish. Stir to blend thoroughly. Fill a deep stock pot with water and add the onion, bay leaf and peppercorns. Bring liquid to a boil over high heat. When boiling, reduce heat and allow to simmer.

To test sausage seasoning, poach a spoonful of the mixture in the simmering water, then taste. Adjust seasoning accordingly.

Lay approximately 2 feet of plastic wrap on a flat surface. Spoon or pipe a line of the sausage mixture across the wrap, starting 1 inch from either side and 2 inches from the bottom of the wrap. Roll the sausage up tightly in the plastic wrap, tying both ends closed.

Place the sausage in simmering water and poach for 10 minutes or until firm. Remove it from the water and drain it in a colander. Carefully unwrap the sausage and drain it again, this time on a paper towel.

Slice on the bias, approximately ½" thick. Overlap four slices on each of four serving plates, with Cayenne Beurre Blanc covering half and pooling on the plate. (Sausage can also be served at room temperature or chilled with an herbed mayonnaise.)

Cayenne Beurre Blanc

2 shallots, peeled and chopped
1 bay leaf
3 cups softened salted butter
2 tablespoons fresh lemon juice
2 tablespoons white wine vinegar
½ cup dry white wine
Pinch of white pepper
Cayenne pepper to taste

Place shallots, bay leaf and 4 tablespoons of butter in a non-reactive saucepan over medium heat. Sauté for 2 minutes or until shallots are translucent. Add lemon juice, vinegar, wine, and white pepper and cook over medium heat for 5 minutes or until the liquid is reduced by half.

Lower heat and whisk in the remaining butter, a bit at a time, being careful not to overheat. When all butter has been incorporated, strain. Season with either black or cayenne pepper to taste. Keep warm in a container over warm water until ready to use.

Crawfish Imperial

Makes 4 servings.

New Orleans is known world wide for its fine restaurants, and for generations one family, the Brennan's, have had a large part in building that reputation. Indeed, many people say that New Orleans' finest cuisine comes about when one branch of the Brennans determines to outdo another, dueling restaurants and family food feuds where every skirmish is a gourmet's delight.

It took a bit of pleading with old friend Ella Brennan, but I managed to pry loose for you, dear reader, this recipe for her family's Commander's Palace restaurant's version of Herbed Duchess Potatoes.

BORDER
5 potatoes (peeled, quartered and boiled)
3 eggs
8 ounces cream
2 ounces butter
3 tablespoons fresh herbs: basil, thyme, oregano (chopped)
Salt and pepper to taste

Use a mixer with its whip attachment and process the potatoes. Add the eggs and butter. Slowly add cream while whipping. When smooth and creamy add herbs and season. Pipe the border onto four oven-safe plates and set aside.

FILLING
6 ounces peppers, green, red and yellow (dice small)
6 ounces onions (dice small)

3 ounces green onion tops (sliced)
1 pound crawfish tails
1 ounce Seafood seasoning
4 ounces fish veloute
2 ounces heavy cream
1 ounce butter (clarified)

Sauté peppers and onions until soft. Add crawfish. Add veloute and seasoning. Finish with cream. Fill plates within the border of potatoes and finish under the broiler to brown potatoes.

Garnish with julienne peppers and whole boiled crawfish.

PUBLICATIONS AND ASSOCIATIONS

Louisiana Crawfish Dealers Directory
Office of Marketing—Crawfish Research and Promotion Board
Louisiana Department of Agriculture and Forestry
P.O. Box 3334
Baton Rouge, LA 70821-3334
PH (504) 922-1280
FAX (504) 922-1289

Crawfish Newsletter
Aquaculture News
P.O. Box 497
Crowley, LA 70527-0497
PH (318) 788-7547
FAX (318) 788-7568

Crawfish Association (Louisiana)
Louisiana Crawfish Farmers Association
Rt. 1, Box 25
Morse, LA 70559-9705

Crawfish Association (South Carolina)
South Carolina Crawfish Growers Association
215 Stockton Road
Rembert, SC 29128

Crawfish Association (International)
International Association of Astacology
c/o Professor Jay Huner
P.O. Box 44650
USL Station
Lafayette, LA 70504

Soft-Shell Crawfish
Louisiana Soft-Shell Crawfish Association
P.O. Box 44509
Lafayette, LA 70504-4509

CRAWFISH SUPPLIERS

Cajun Spices, Books and Souvenirs (Retail)
Louisiana Catalog
Highway 1 @ W 70th, Bayouside
Cut Off, LA 70345
PH (800) 375-4100 or (504) 632-4100
FAX (504) 632-4129

Scandinavian Foods, Books and Souvenirs (Retail)
Anderson Butik
P.O. Box 151
Lindsborg, Kansas 67456
PH (800) 782-4132 or (913) 227-2183
FAX (913) 227-3268

Biological Specimens (live or preserved)
Atchafalaya Biological Supply
832 St. Phillip Street
Raceland, LA 70394
PH (504) 537-3135

Cooked Crawfish (Heat and Serve)
Robin's Restaurant
P.O. Box 542
Henderson, LA 70517
PH (318) 228-7594

LIVE CRAWFISH SHIPPED ANYWHERE
Many more suppliers of live, cooked and/or peeled crawfish are listed in the dealers directory of the Louisiana Crawfish Promotion and Research Board. A list of soft-shell crawfish dealers is available through the Louisiana Soft-Shell Crawfish Association.

Bayou Land Seafood
1008 Vincent Berard Road
Breaux Bridge, LA 70517
PH (318) 667-6119
FAX (318) 667-6059

Boulet Export
P.O. Box 787
Larose, LA 70373
PH (504) 798-7697
FAX (504) 798-7678

Jake's Famous Crawfish and Seafood
P.O. Box 97
Clackamus, OR 97015
PH (503) 657-1892
FAX (503) 655-8166

Northern Crayfish Company
P.O. Box 482
Chetek, WI 54728
PH (715) 924-2143

CRAWFISH EVENTS

Breaux Bridge (Louisiana) Crawfish Festival.
First full weekend in May. Est. 1959. East of Lafayette, southwest of Baton Rouge, two hours from New Orleans. Oldest, largest crawfish festival in Louisiana, for a time second in size only to Mardi Gras among state's celebrations. Food, music, boat parade, crawfish races, and many, many other activities. Contact: Breaux Bridge Crawfish Festival, P.O. Box 25, Breaux Bridge, LA 70517; PH (318) 332-6655.

International Symposium on Freshwater Crayfish.
Held every two years. Est. 1972. Host nation rotates. For those seriously interested in crawfish and their aquaculture, this is the place to be. Contact: International Association of Astacology, c/o Professor Jay Huner, P.O. Box 44650, USL Station, Lafayette, LA 70504.

Louisiana Crawfish Festival.
First weekend in April, four-day event. Est. 1977. In St. Bernard Parish, just east of New Orleans; host town rotates. Large festival, food, music, rides, crawfish races. Contact: Louisiana State Tourism Office, 529 St. Ann St, New Orleans, LA 70116; PH (504) 277-9552.

Ragin' Cajun Crawfish Festival and Gumbo Cook-off.
April. Est. 1983 in Memphis; Est. 1987 in Little Rock. Riverfront parks in both cities. Crawfish race, eating contest and *bobbing for live crawfish!* For information on either city's festival, contact: Crawfish Festival, 47 North 3rd, Memphis, TN 38103; (901) 526-4395.

Sorrento (Louisiana) Crawfish Festival.
Mid-May. Est. 1991. On the Mississippi River between New Orleans and Baton
Rouge. Crawfish cooked every way. Contact: Mr. Fern Barnett, P.O. Box 207,
Sorrento, LA 70778; (504) 675-5355.

South Carolina Crawfish Festival and Aquaculture Fair.
Last weekend in April. Est. 1981. At Pawley's Island, on the coast between
Georgetown and Myrtle Beach. Crawfish dishes, crawfish races, crawfish-eating
contests. Contact: S.C. Crawfish Festival, P.O. Box 598, Pawley's Island, SC
29585; PH (803) 237-0147.

Texas Crawfish Festival.
Last weekend in April. Est. 1987. Spring, Texas, just north of Houston. Food,
games and four stages of music (Country and western, Cajun, Zydeco, Rhythm and
blues) with dance floors! Contact: Spring Preservation League, 123F Midway,
Spring, Texas 77373; (713) 353-9310.

Tualatin (Oregon) Crawfish Festival.
Second Saturday in August. Est. 1951, oldest crawfish festival in U.S. Tualatin
Community Park, ten miles south of Portland on I-5. Two stages live entertain-
ment, parade, bike race, dog show, food, rides, crafts, and a crawfish-eating contest.
Contact: Tualatin Chamber of Commerce, P.O. Box 701 Tualatin, Oregon 97062;
(503) 692-0780.

World Championship Crawfish Etouffée Cook-off.
Last Sunday in March. Est. 1986. Downtown Eunice, Louisiana, one hour northwest of Lafayette. Open competition, awards given. For one dollar each, public may
sample one hundred versions of the classic dish. Cajun music. Contact: Eunice
Chamber of Commerce, P.O. Box 508, Eunice, LA 70535; PH (318) 457-2565.

FURTHER READING

Akin, Johnnye. *The Crawfish Cookbook: Cajun, Creole, and Selected Recipes.* Baton Rouge: Claitor's, 1986.

Ancelet, B., J. Edwards, and G. Pitre. *Cajun Country.* Jackson: University Press of Mississippi, 1991.

Avault, James, and others, eds. *Freshwater Crayfish: Papers from the International Symposia.* 8 vols. Various publishers, under the auspices of International Association of Astacology Secretariat, Lafayette, La., 1972–91.

Botkin, B. A. *A Treasury of Mississippi River Folklore.* New York: American Legacy Press, 1955.

Brasseaux, Carl. *The Founding of New Acadia.* Baton Rouge: Louisiana State University Press, 1987.

Brunnings, Florence. *Folk Song Index.* New York: Garland Publishing, 1981.

Bush, Charles (director). *Crawfish!* Baton Rouge: Bush Films, 1987.

Calala, L. *Crawfish: Keeping Crawfish for Bait, Making Softshell Crawfish and Their Care.* New London, Ohio: Calala's Water Haven, 1976.

Collin, Rima and Richard. *The New Orleans Cookbook.* New York: Knopf, 1979.

Comeaux, Malcolm. *Atchafalaya Swamp Life.* Baton Rouge: Louisiana State University School of Geoscience, 1972.

Courtine, Robert. *The Hundred Glories of French Cooking.* New York: Farrar, Straus, Giroux, 1973.

Douglas, Alfred. *The Tarot: Origins, Meanings and Use of the Cards.* New York: Penguin, 1983.

Edler, Tim. *Crawfish-Man . . .* Baton Rouge: Little Cajun Books.
Adventures of Crawfish-Man. 1978.

Crawfish-Man Rescues Ron Guidry. 1979.

Crawfish-Man's Night Befo' Christmas. 1984.

Crawfish-Man Rescues the Ole Beachcomber. 1985.

Fontenot, Mary Alice. *Clovis Crawfish . . .* Gretna, La.: Pelican Publishing.

Clovis Crawfish and Etienne Escargot. 1979.

Clovis Crawfish and the Singing Cigales. 1981.

Clovis Crawfish and the Orphan Zo-Zo. 1983.

Clovis Crawfish and Petit Papillon. 1984.

Clovis Crawfish and His Friends. 1985.

Clovis Crawfish and the Curious Crapaud. 1986.

Clovis Crawfish and the Spinning Spider. 1987.

Clovis Crawfish and the Big Bétail. 1988.

Clovis Crawfish and Michelle Mantis. 1989.

Clovis Crawfish and Simeon Suce-Fleur. 1990.

Clovis Crawfish and Bertile's Bon Voyage. 1991.

Franklin, Stephen. *Origins of the Tarot Deck.* Jefferson, N.C.: McFarland, 1988.

Guiterrez, C. Paige. *Cajun Foodways.* Jackson: University Press of Mississippi, 1992.

Esman, Marjorie R. *The Town That Crawfish Built.* Baton Rouge: VAAPR, Inc., 1984.

Frazer, Sir James. *The Golden Bough: The Roots of Religion and Folklore.* New York: Avenel Books, 1981.

Gerber, Adolph. *Great Russian Animal Tales.* Baltimore: Modern Language Association of America, 1891.

Grandville, J. J. *Bizarries and Fantasies of Grandville.* New York: Dover Publications, 1974.

Groves, Roy. *The Crawfish: Its Nature and Nurture.* Farnham, Surrey, England: Fishing News Books, 1985.

Hart, C. W., Jr., and Janice Clark. *An Interdisciplinary Bibliography of Freshwater Crayfishes.* Washington, D.C.: Smithsonian Institution Press, 1989.

Hearne, Lafcadio. *Creole Cookbook.* Gretna, La.: Pelican Publishing, 1990.

Holdich, D. M., and R. S. Lowery, eds. *Freshwater Crayfish: Biology, Management, and Exploitation.* Portland, Ore.: Timber Press, 1991.

Hughes, Robert. *The Fatal Shore.* New York: Knopf, 1986.

Huner, Jay, and J. E. Barr. *Red Swamp Crawfish: Biology and Exploitation*. Baton Rouge: Center for Wetlands Resources, 1991.

Huner, Jay, and Evan Brown. *Crustacean and Mollusk Aquaculture in the U.S.* Westport, Conn.: AVI Publishing Company, 1985.

Huxley, Thomas H. *The Crayfish. An Introduction to Zoology*. New York: Appleton & Co., 1880. (numerous later editions)

Jones, Ernest. *The Life and Work of Sigmund Freud*. New York: Doubleday, 1961.

Jumonville, Betty, and Jay Mounger. *The Louisiana Crawfish Cookbook*. Austin: Hart Graphics, 1984.

Kropottan, Alexander. *Best of Russian Cooking*. New York: Charles Scribner's Sons, 1964.

La Fontaine, Jean de. *Fables*. New York: Dutton, 1909.

———. *Fables of La Fontaine*. New York: Viking, 1954.

Lankford, George, ed. *Native American Legends*. Little Rock: August House, 1987.

Lomax, Alan, and John Lomax. *American Ballads and Folksongs*. New York: Macmillan, 1934.

———. *Best Loved American Folksongs*. New York: Grosset & Dunlop, 1947.

Madara, Jerry. *102 Uses for a Louisiana Crawfish*. Baton Rouge: Gleason Publishing, 1984.

Magyar, Elek. *The Gourmet's Cookbook*. Budapest: Corvina, 1970.

Olszewski, Peter. *A Salute to the Humble Yabby*. Sydney, Australia: Angus and Robertson, 1980.

Root, Waverly. *The Food of France*. New York: Knopf, 1958.

Sadovnikov, D. *Riddles of the Russian People*. Ann Arbor: Ardes, 1986.

Saxon, Lyle, Edward Dreyer, and Robert Tallant. *Gumbo Ya-Ya: Folktales of Louisiana*. Gretna, La.: Pelican Publishing, 1991.

Schwabe, Calvin. *Unmentionable Cuisine*. Richmond: University of Virginia Press, 1979.

Silber, Irwin and Fred. *Folksinger's Wordbook*. New York: Oak, 1973.

Spotte, S. *Seawater Aquariums: The Captive Environment*. New York: John Wiley and Sons, 1979.

Swanton, John. *Indian Tribes of the Lower Mississippi Valley and Adjacent Coast of the Gulf of Mexico*. Washington, D.C.: Bureau of American Ethnology, Smithsonian Institution, 1911.

Swanton, John. *Myths and Tales of the Southeastern Indians.* Washington, D.C.:
Bureau of American Ethnology, Smithsonian Institution, 1929.

A Teacher's Guide to Crayfish: Investigating the Behavior of a Freshwater Animal. New
York: McGraw-Hill, 1976.

Thompson, Stith. *Motif-Index of Folk-Literature.* 6 vols. Bloomington: Indiana
University Press, 1932–36.

Umiker-Seabeok, Jean, and Thomas Seabeok, eds. *Aboriginal Sign Languages of the
Americas and Australia.* New York and London: Plenum Press, 1978.

Wallis, Hal (producer) and Michael Curtis (director). *King Creole.* 1958.

Young, James. *The Toadstool Millionaires.* Princeton, N.J.: Princeton University
Press, 1961.

INDEX

INDEX